INDUSTRY 4.0
REVOLUTION

How Startups Empower Digital Transformation in Industries?

AEKNATH MISHRA

Industry 4.0 Revolution

Inside Steel & Aluminium Industries

How Startups Empower Digital Transformation in Industries

Aeknath Mishra

Innovation with AI, IIoT, ML, Automation, Robotics and Technology

DEDICATED TO

This book is dedicated to His Highness Sheikh Mohamed bin Zayed Al Nahyan, President of the UAE and Ruler of Abu Dhabi.

His visionary leadership drives the UAE's progress in AI and advanced technologies, as exemplified by the inauguration of the AIATC and the launch of MGX, spearheading global technological innovation for the betterment of future generations.

ACKNOWLEDGEMENTS

Throughout the process of writing this book, several individuals provided invaluable assistance in editing, proofreading, cover design, and interior formatting, as well as offering consistent support. I would like to express my gratitude to Angie Alaya for her creative contribution to the cover design and to Will for his meticulous work on interior formatting.

Special thanks to my friend Jatin for his technical editing expertise; Jatin spent countless hours editing, proofreading, and helping to craft my "digital transformation" voice.

I would also like to extend my heartfelt thanks to Sergey Sir, Iman Ma'am, John, and Chris Sir for their unwavering support and encouragement.

Additionally, I would like to acknowledge my daughter Tamanna for her domain expertise in computer science, artificial intelligence, and API files; without your continued support, none of this would have been possible.

Thank you all for your contributions and for believing in this project.

The views published in this book are my own and do not represent the intellectual property or opinion of any organization.

CONTENTS

Introduction 13
Startup-Led Digital Navigation 16
Evolution of Industry 4.0 24
Understanding Digital Transformation 41
Embracing Automation and Robotics 46
Leveraging IoT and Predictive Analytics 51
Power of Data Analytics 56
Supply Chain Optimization 61
Digital Twin Technology Exploration 66
Cloud computing: the game changer 72
Blockchain revolutionizes supply chain 76
AR and VR technology 81
Smart manufacturing for factories 86
Empowering digital workforce 93
Transformation challenges and solutions 98
Future trends and sustainable growth 103
Case Studies of Transformation 108
Startup's Role in Manufacturing 114
Book Pitch 126
Assessment for Industry 4.0 129
Evaluating Digital Transformation Needs 133
Digital Transformation Resources 137
About the Author 149
References 151
Books By Aeknath Mishra 155

INTRODUCTION

This era is of rapid technological advancement, sustainable growth and digital innovation; thus, metal manufacturing is undergoing a profound transformation. Industry 4.0, often termed the Fourth Industrial Revolution, heralds a new age of connectivity, automation, and data-driven decision-making. "Industry 4.0 Revolution: How Startups Empower Digital Transformation in Industries" explores the intersection of technology and manufacturing, unraveling the complexities and opportunities ahead. This book examines how startup trends propel the global economy to prominence, driven by youthful dynamism and entrepreneurial zeal. Startups complement the traditional industry's relentless drive, fostering collaborative efforts that lead to global excellence in the digital age. This journey highlights the symbiotic relationship transforming modern manufacturing.

When electric power first appeared on the scene, people were suspicious. The promise of an uninterrupted supply of light and power was bewitching, and the invention of the electric light bulb threatened the oil monopoly. Unlike firewood, electricity was easy to use, available during all seasons, and, most importantly, safe from recurring accidents. Electricity's quick win to light up homes also warmed people's hearts, leading to improved productivity, increased income, fewer accidents, and a dramatically improved quality of life. As people experienced these benefits, they were willing to embrace other applications of electric power, gradually shifting away from oil.

Digital technology is now experiencing similar transitional challenges. Just as electric power prevailed, digital transformation will too. However, this transformation is not a regular train journey but a long roller-coaster ride, initially making first-timers dizzy and scared. To embrace this change, one must hold on, face the fear, and enjoy the ride, understanding that the process is time-consuming but ultimately worthwhile.

This book, "Industry 4.0 Revolution: How Startups Empower Digital Transformation in Industries," delves into the digital revolution, providing a brief history of digital transformation, distinguishing between digitization and digitalization, and exploring their implications for business process reengineering and future digital transformations. Understanding these terms is crucial for navigating the digital transformation of industrial business models.

Implementing technologies into business processes is only part of the journey. These technologies must add value for customers, businesses, and stakeholders. Success in digital transformation requires reshaping customer value propositions and transforming operations using digital technologies for better customer interaction and collaboration. This book defines digital transformation as a sustainable, company-level transformation in aluminium and steel manufacturing industries through revised or newly created business operations and models. This transformation, achieved via value-added digitization initiatives, ultimately results in improved profitability.

As the world becomes increasingly interconnected, the traditional paradigms of manufacturing are evolving at an unprecedented pace. From smart factories equipped with IoT sensors to predictive analytics driving operational efficiency, every aspect of the manufacturing process is being reimagined and reinvented. Here, we delve deep into the realms of digital transformation, shedding light on the transformative technologies and strategies shaping the future of integrated metal manufacturing complexes.

Moreover, as the manufacturing sector undergoes rapid digitization and automation, the startup ecosystem plays a crucial role in driving innovation, disruption, and sustainability. Startups are at the forefront of developing breakthrough technologies and pioneering new business models that challenge traditional norms and unlock untapped opportunities. From AI-powered predictive maintenance solutions to blockchain-enabled supply chain traceability platforms, startups are revolutionizing the manufacturing industry by offering agile, scalable, and cost-effective solutions. In the core of this book, we will delve into the role, responsibility, and opportunities presented by the startup ecosystem, highlighting the collaborative potential between established manufacturers and innovative startups to fuel growth and drive positive change.

Drawing upon real-world examples, case studies, and expert insights, "Industry 4.0 Revolution" serves as a comprehensive guide for industry professionals, policymakers, and academics navigating the complexities of Industry 4.0.

Join us on an enlightening journey to unravel the mysteries of Industry 4.0 and discover the boundless opportunities that await in the realm of manufacturing. Under the urging of world bodies to fulfill sustainable compliances, this transformation is not just about technology but also about responsibility to future generations. Together, let us explore how Industry 4.0 and the startup ecosystem are shaping the future of our interconnected world, paving the way for innovations that will sustain and empower the generations yet to come.

STARTUP-LED DIGITAL NAVIGATION

How to read each chapter?

Evolution of Industry 4.0:

Dive into the fascinating world of Industry 4.0, tracing its roots, history and evolution. Explore key concepts and principles shaping the future of manufacturing, and understand why Industry 4.0 is indispensable in today's industrial landscape.

Understanding Digital Transformation in Manufacturing:

Unravel the concept of digital transformation and its profound impact on manufacturing processes. Discover the drivers and enablers of digital transformation, and gain insights into its transformative effects on operations.

Embracing Automation and Robotics:

Explore the pivotal role of automation and robotics in modern manufacturing. Delve into different types of robotic applications, weigh their benefits against challenges, and understand how they revolutionize production.

Leveraging IoT and Predictive Analytics:

Step into the world of the Internet of Things (IoT) and predictive analytics in operations, where data-driven decisions reign supreme. Learn how IoT applications optimize manufacturing processes and how predictive analytics ensures proactive maintenance and optimization.

Harnessing the Power of Data Analytics:

Unlock the potential of data analytics in manufacturing. Discover techniques for data collection, data cleaning and analysis, and understand how business intelligence derived from data drives strategic decision-making.

Supply Chain Optimization in the Digital Age:

Explore the evolution of supply chain management and the challenges faced by traditional supply chains. Discover digital solutions that optimize supply chain operations and enhance efficiency in the digital age.

Exploring Digital Twin Technology:

Enter the realm of digital twin technology, where virtual replicas transform manufacturing. Learn about its components, applications, and the promising future it holds for the industry.

Cloud Computing for Manufacturing Excellence:

Embark on a journey into the cloud, where manufacturing operations are revolutionized and in real time. Understand the fundamentals of cloud computing, its deployment models, and its myriad applications in manufacturing.

Blockchain Integration in Supply Chains:

Delve into the world of blockchain technology and its transformative potential in supply chain management. Explore real-world applications, advantages, and the challenges of blockchain integration.

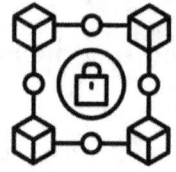

Augmented Reality and Virtual Reality Applications in Manufacturing:

Immerse yourself in the world of AR, VR and MR technologies, where reality is augmented and virtual. Discover their applications in training, maintenance, and design, and envision future trends.

Smart Manufacturing and Interconnected Production Systems:

Navigate the landscape of smart manufacturing, where interconnected systems drive efficiency. Explore the components of smart factories, implementation challenges, and the keys to success.

Empowering the Digital Workforce:

Learn about the critical role of digital skills in manufacturing and the strategies for empowering the workforce. Discover Safety, Health, Wellbeing, training and development programs that foster engagement and adoption of digital technologies.

Overcoming Challenges in Digital Transformation:

Identify common challenges in digital transformation and explore strategies for overcoming resistance. Draw inspiration from successful case studies and learn best practices for navigating the transformation journey.

Future Trends and Innovations in Manufacturing:

Peer into the future of manufacturing and anticipate emerging trends and innovations. Explore the potential impact of new technologies on the industry and prepare for the next wave of innovation.

Case Studies:

Real-World Examples of Successful Digital Transformation in Manufacturing. Dive into real-world case studies from various industries, showcasing successful digital transformation initiatives. Extract valuable insights, implementation strategies, and best practices for your own transformation journey.

Future Trends, Opportunities in Manufacturing, and Startup Ecosystem:

Discover future trends and opportunities in manufacturing, with a focus on the role of the startup ecosystem. Explore collaborative opportunities between startups and established manufacturers, driving innovation and growth.

Startup's Revolutionizing Digital Transmission

To revolutionize digital transformation (DT) implementation, industries must embrace the startup ecosystem and collaborate with visionary leaders on critical challenges to achieve desired results. Collaboration with the best ecosystem partners, including startup founders and visionary leaders, is essential. Balancing both short- and long-term targets is crucial in driving rapid change while keeping sight of the larger vision. Sustainable manufacturing, digital twins, and the convergence of cyber-physical systems are reshaping the future of manufacturing. Small manufacturers and startups are leveraging accessible technologies like cloud computing and open-source software to compete with larger incumbents, fostering innovation and collaboration. Here are 14 current startups making waves in the metal manufacturing industry:

1. **Transformation in Manufacturing: Celestial Manufacturing Solutions** - Pioneers in implementing sustainable manufacturing practices by integrating circular economy principles and renewable energy sources. Example - www.h2greensteel.com – Powering a new, clean industrial revolution.

2. **Automation and Robotics: Cobot Auto Tech** - Specializes in deploying collaborative robots (cobots) for precision tasks in metal manufacturing, enhancing efficiency and safety. Example - www.anybotics.com - Increased uptime and improved preventive maintenance through asset health monitoring.

3. **Predictive Analytics: Predicti Tech** - Provides advanced predictive maintenance solutions using IoT sensors and machine learning to foresee equipment failures and optimize maintenance schedules. Example - www.facilio.com - IoT Intelligence that seamlessly fits into your existing stack.

4. **Power of Data Analytics: Data Matrix** - Harnesses big data analytics to offer actionable insights for operational efficiency and strategic decision-making in metal production. Example - www.mavenintel.com - Transforming Insights into Operations.

5. **Supply Chain Optimization: Logic Chain** - Utilizes blockchain and AI to ensure transparency, efficiency, transactions and real-time

tracking in the supply chain, reducing waste and costs. Example - www.synox.io - The Internet of Things (IoT), Artificial Intelligence (AI) and blockchain are three technologies that are constantly being used in Supply Chain 4.0 and the logistics industry.

6. **Digital Twin Technology: Emirates Twin Makers** - Develops digital twin solutions that create virtual replicas of manufacturing processes, enabling real-time monitoring and optimization. Example - www.intemic.com – Lets your data working for you, makes a data-driven platform that digitizes and optimizes production operations and processes. It allows manufacturers to create digital twins of manufacturing equipment and simulate its performance in different operating environments, reducing the need for physical testing. The platform utilizes AI and simulation models to understand, predict, and make decisions by correlating data from production, quality control, and logistics.

7. **Cloud Computing for Manufacturing: Cloud Fab** - Offers cloud-based manufacturing solutions that facilitate real-time data access, collaboration, and operational excellence. Example - www.rapyder.com – Build Better, Faster: Cloud Solutions For Manufacturing Industry.

8. **Blockchain Integration in Supply Chains: Blockcom Supply** - Enhances supply chain traceability and security using blockchain technology, ensuring ethical sourcing and regulatory compliance. Example - www.scorechain.com - a global leader in Blockchain compliance, offering automated AML/CFT solutions that integrate seamlessly into your workflows. Ensure data privacy and comply with regulatory requirements and preemptively detect risks with our advanced analytics.

9. **AR, VR & MR in Manufacturing: Virtual Fab** - Innovates with augmented and virtual reality applications for training, maintenance, and design, improving productivity and reducing

errors. Example - www.aruvr.com – transforms manufacturing, transform your approach.

10. **Interconnected Production Systems: Smart Grid Systems** - Implements interconnected production systems to streamline operations, increase efficiency, and foster responsive manufacturing environments. Example - www.discover.aveva.com - With AVEVA Unified Operations Center, you can converge and visualize a combination of production metrics, maintenance analytics, engineering documentation, financial performance or anything in between.

11. **Digital Workforce: Skill Shift** - Empowers the digital workforce through comprehensive training programs, face recognition for mood and attendance in Industry 4.0 technologies, fostering engagement and adoption. Example - www.daon.com - facial authentication is designed to provide maximum security.

12. **Cyber Threats in Digital Transformation: Cyber Guard** - Provides robust cyber security solutions to protect manufacturing systems from digital threats, ensuring secure and resilient operations. Example - www.orro.group.com – Our security methodologies by moving towards a more holistic, risk-based approach that includes threat intelligence, user behavior analytics, and AI/ML-based technologies.

13. **Energy Plus** - Focuses on enhancing energy efficiency and emission control, using advanced analytics and IoT to optimize resource utilization and reduce carbon footprints. Example - www.greensoftware.foundation - Research, tools, code, libraries, and training for building applications that emit less carbon into our atmosphere has been managed by open source working group in the green software foundation.

14. **Green Cycle** - Innovates in producing high-quality recycled Aluminium, reducing energy consumption and promoting

sustainability through advanced impurity extraction technologies. Example - www.hydro.com - To reach the Paris climate agreement and keep the global temperature increase below 1.5 degrees, we need to decarbonize energy systems, produce for circularity, and recycle resources already in use.

The metal manufacturing industry is on the cusp of a digital revolution, fueled by collaborations between startups and established manufacturers. By adopting innovative technologies and sustainable practices, the industry can reach new heights of efficiency, productivity, and environmental stewardship. Strategic partnerships and the integration of advanced solutions position the metal manufacturing sector to spearhead a future characterized by digital transformation and sustainable growth.

EVOLUTION OF INDUSTRY 4.0

Introduction to industry 4.0: Dive into the fascinating world of Industry 4.0, tracing its roots and evolution. Explore key concepts and principles shaping the future of manufacturing, and understand why Industry 4.0 is indispensable in today's industrial landscape.

- *Definition and Evolution of Industry 4.0*
- *Key Concepts and Principles*
- *Importance of Industry 4.0 in Manufacturing*

INDUSTRY 4.0 REVOLUTION

In the modern era of rapid technological advancement and digital innovation, the term "Industry 4.0" has become ubiquitous in the manufacturing landscape. This revolution, often referred to as the Fourth Industrial Revolution, represents a fundamental shift in the way goods are produced, and processes are optimized. In this comprehensive exploration of Industry 4.0, we will delve into its definition, evolution, key concepts, and the pivotal role it plays in shaping the future of manufacturing. In recent years, there have been several trends and technologies in metal manufacturing that have Industry 4.0, coined in Germany as "Industrie 4.0," refers to the convergence of digital technologies with traditional manufacturing processes to create smart, interconnected systems. It represents a paradigm emerged to change the face of this industry. These include automation and robotics, 3D printing, computer-aided design and manufacturing, additive manufacturing, advanced materials, and the integration of IoT and Industry 4.0 technologies. These developments have led to increased efficiency, precision, cost-effectiveness, and the ability to create complex and unique designs in the industry. As these trends continue to evolve and improve by 2030, we can expect to see even greater advancements in the heavy metal industry in the future.

Definition and Evolution of Industry 4.0

The manufacturing process is shifting towards automation, data exchange, and the Internet of Things (IoT) in industrial settings. This shift builds upon previous industrial revolutions, namely the mechanization of manufacturing (Industry 1.0), mass production (Industry 2.0), and automation through electronics and IT (Industry 3.0).

The evolution of Industry 4.0 can be traced back to the early 2010s when advancements in technologies such as cloud computing, artificial intelligence (AI), and IoT began to converge with manufacturing processes. This convergence marked the beginning of a new era characterized by cyber-physical systems, where machines communicate and collaborate with each other autonomously.

The metals industry is under significant pressure to transform due to environmental, political, and cultural factors. In 2024, metal manufacturing industries are setting ambitious goals for energy management, emission control, increased productivity, uptime, operational cost control, and optimized capacity. A complete paradigm shift through digital transformation initiatives is necessary to achieve these goals.

Eager to attract the next generation of digitally literate talent concerned with climate change, companies are demonstrating their commitment to sustainability and innovation. To revolutionize digital transformation (DT) implementation, industries must embrace the startup ecosystem and collaborate with visionary leaders on critical challenges to achieve desired results.

This book provides insights into how metal industries are transitioning from conventional to modern, safe, smart, and sustainable operations. Here are the processes by which heavy metal producers envision digital and sustainable productions:

Powerful, Integrated Solutions: Speeding up decarbonization.
New Business Models: Ensuring value outcomes and competitiveness.
Autonomous Operations: Enhancing transparency across value chains.

No single company can achieve this alone. Collaboration with the best ecosystem partners, including startup founders and visionary leaders, is essential. Balancing both short- and long-term targets is crucial in driving rapid change while keeping sight of the larger vision.

Business leaders in metal industries need organization-wide visibility and control. Genuine efforts, rather than symbolic actions to satisfy international compliance agencies and customers, are necessary. This includes quickly evaluating production impacts due to rising material costs, adapting pricing strategies, and better managing supply chains and assets. Data integration at all levels—from equipment and processes to engineering and business systems—is a core business imperative.

Metal producers generate a lot of data but struggle to make it valuable for digital applications. Real-time, affordable communication between the cloud and the shop floor is essential. Digital applications require trusted data; otherwise, they cause unnecessary noise and distractions.

Converging operational, IT, and engineering data is challenging, especially with heterogeneous information systems. Many metal plants have incompatible legacy OT systems, which can be a significant hurdle. The integration process requires domain expertise and specific connectivity solutions.

Tech-savvy startup founders have the right combination of domain-specific expertise and knowledge of both OT and IT infrastructure. They ensure that industrial data management approaches are aligned with business strategies to positively impact the bottom line. This involves labeling, modeling, and structuring industry-specific data, and managing high volumes of data securely and cost-effectively.

The best way forward is to discard old practices and embrace the new digital transformation journey. When basic data requirements are met, numerous potential use cases open up, which will be discussed in the proceeding chapters. The focus will be on improving existing equipment availability and optimizing processes to run at optimal and profitable levels.

Operational assets and process optimization must be treated separately. The real value comes from uncovering hidden relationships, tracing spam data buildup, and linking correlations through new DT utilization. This requires leadership confidence and stakeholder engagement.

Industry 4.0 and the startup ecosystem help digital transformation teams improve interactions across the value chain, engaging people in real-time towards common goals. This knowledge enables operations personnel to manage resources in real-time and deliver contracted product quantities and qualities faster.

Industrial Analytics and AI Enable Deeper Insights: Companies focused on continuous improvement are eager to explore how enterprise-grade industrial analytics and AI can provide deeper insights into activities, asset or process behavior, leading to higher productivity, lower energy consumption, lower emissions, and better industry reputation. Leaders seek real-time visibility into their business, regardless of location or time.

When lacking in-house expertise, metal producers turn to startup founders for fast access to cyber security services, predictive maintenance, critical equipment or process performance optimization, and shared risks. Technology leaders want to see plants adopt new solutions, but the digital landscape can be intimidating.

Decision-makers in metal companies must be convinced that technology applications will deliver measurable results. This book includes real-life examples demonstrating the value of digital transformation strategies in the metals industry. The seven digital solution areas representing value pillars are:

- *Leadership Confidence*: Empower leaders with comprehensive data and insights to make informed decisions and drive organizational success.

- *Operational Excellence*: Achieve flexibility, value chain visibility, and consistent strategy execution for optimal performance.

- *Process Performance*: Enhance quality and throughput while minimizing variability and lead time.

- *Asset Performance*: Maximize uptime and minimize maintenance costs through effective asset management.

- *Sustainability Solutions*: Ensure compliance reporting and reduce resource costs and risks.

- *Connected Worker*: Improve safety and productivity while preserving and sharing valuable knowledge.

- *Cyber Security*: Protect critical systems and data with robust security measures.

INDUSTRY 4.0 REVOLUTION

Digital transformation discussions between process industry leaders, technology implementors, and innovators will continue. Increased complexity requires mastery of different technologies, industry-specific processes, and cyber security, providing consultancy and assistance from design to system maintenance.

Adopting digital solutions leads to better performance at reduced capital costs, standardizing operational, process, maintenance, environmental, and supply chain management practices. Startups establish a single source of truth for all information, strengthening continuous improvement cycles.

With energy cost, efficiency, and environmental implications gaining top priority globally, new digital tools are developed rapidly in collaboration with customers, universities, and ecosystem players. The most important aspect across all digital solution areas is cyber security. Leading metals customers on the digital transformation path take a proactive security approach, periodically reviewing strategies and performing simulations under different circumstances.

Deploying digital applications on various platforms ensures intellectual property protection and comprehensive cyber security. The Cyber Security Reference Architecture aligns with current standards and best practices.

Latest digital services have improved the cyber security of industrial sites globally. Many customers schedule risk assessments as part of annual service agreements, while others use cyber security analytics dashboards for continuous monitoring and issue resolution.

Key Concepts and Principles

At the core of Industry 4.0 lie several key concepts and principles that drive its implementation and adoption in manufacturing:

- *Interconnectivity*: Industry 4.0 emphasizes the seamless integration and connectivity of machines, sensors, and systems across the entire value chain. This interconnectedness enables real-time data exchange and collaboration, fostering agility and responsiveness in manufacturing operations.

- *Data Transparency*: Central to Industry 4.0 is the generation, collection, and analysis of vast amounts of data from manufacturing processes. This data transparency enables manufacturers to gain valuable insights into their operations, identify inefficiencies, and make informed decisions to optimize performance.

- *Automation and Robotics*: Automation plays a central role in Industry 4.0, with robotics and intelligent systems taking over repetitive and labor-intensive tasks. Robotic arms, automated guided vehicles (AGVs), and cobots (collaborative robots) work alongside human operators to enhance efficiency and productivity on the factory floor.

- *Advanced Analytics and AI*: Industry 4.0 leverages advanced analytics and AI algorithms to derive actionable insights from data. Predictive analytics, machine learning, and cognitive computing enable manufacturers to forecast demand, anticipate maintenance issues, and optimize production schedules in real-time.

- *Smart Factories*: Industry 4.0 envisions the creation of smart factories, where cyber-physical systems monitor and control physical processes autonomously. These smart factories are characterized by flexibility, adaptability, and customization, allowing manufacturers to respond quickly to changing market demands.

Importance of Industry 4.0 in Manufacturing

The adoption of Industry 4.0 principles and technologies holds immense significance for the manufacturing industry, offering a wide range of benefits and opportunities:

- *Enhanced Efficiency and Productivity*: By automating routine tasks and optimizing processes, Industry 4.0 enables manufacturers to achieve higher levels of efficiency and productivity. Real-time monitoring and predictive maintenance minimize downtime, while data-driven insights inform continuous improvement initiatives.

- *Improved Quality and Customization*: Industry 4.0 facilitates the production of high-quality, customized products tailored to individual customer needs. Advanced analytics and AI algorithms identify defects early in the production process, allowing for timely interventions and quality assurance.

- *Cost Reduction and Resource Optimization*: Automation and optimization of manufacturing processes lead to cost savings through reduced labor costs, energy consumption, and material waste. Predictive maintenance prevents costly equipment failures, while supply chain optimization minimizes inventory holding costs.

- *Agility and Adaptability*: Industry 4.0 enables manufacturers to respond quickly to changing market dynamics and customer demands. Smart factories equipped with IoT sensors and interconnected systems can adjust production schedules in real-time, ensuring timely delivery of products and services.

- *Innovation and Competitiveness*: Embracing Industry 4.0 fosters a culture of innovation and continuous improvement within manufacturing organizations. By leveraging emerging technologies and digital solutions, manufacturers can stay ahead of the competition, drive innovation, and seize new market opportunities.

SWOT Analysis

SWOT analysis for Aluminium manufacturing Industries	
Strengths	**Weaknesses**
1. High demand in multiple sectors. 2. Light-weight and durable properties. 3. Recyclability.	1. Energy-intensive extraction processes. 2. Volatility in raw material prices.
Opportunities	**Threats**
1. Expanding into green manufacturing. 2. Diversifying into niche markets like EVs, aerospace, etc.	1. Regulatory changes and environmental concerns. 2. Competition from alternative materials.

SWOT Analysis for Steel Manufacturing Industries

Strengths	Weaknesses
1. High Demand Across Industries: Steel is essential in construction, automotive, infrastructure, and manufacturing, ensuring steady demand. 2. Strength and Durability: Steel offers superior strength and durability, making it ideal for load-bearing and structural applications. 3. Recyclability: Steel can be recycled indefinitely without losing its properties, contributing to sustainability and cost-efficiency. 4. Advanced Manufacturing Techniques: Integration of advanced technologies like automation and AI in steel production enhances efficiency and product quality.	1. Energy-Intensive Production: Steel manufacturing processes, especially those involving blast furnaces, are highly energy-intensive and contribute significantly to carbon emissions. 2. Raw Material Price Volatility: Prices of key raw materials like iron ore and coking coal are subject to significant fluctuations, impacting production costs and profitability. 3. Environmental Impact: Traditional steelmaking processes have a considerable environmental footprint, including air and water pollution, which attracts regulatory scrutiny and public criticism.

Opportunities	Threats
1. Green Steel Manufacturing: Advancements in green technologies, such as hydrogen-based reduction processes, present opportunities to reduce the carbon footprint of steel production. 2. Expansion into High-Tech Sectors: Growing demand for high-strength, lightweight steel in electric vehicles (EVs), aerospace, and renewable energy sectors open up new market opportunities. 3. Digital Transformation: Adoption of Industry 4.0 technologies, such as IoT, predictive analytics, and digital twins, can optimize production processes, reduce downtime, and enhance supply chain efficiency. 4. Emerging Markets: Expansion into developing countries with growing infrastructure needs can drive significant demand for steel products.	1. Regulatory Changes: Stricter environmental regulations and carbon taxes can increase operational costs and require significant investments in cleaner technologies. 2. Competition from Alternative Materials: Advances in composite materials, Aluminium, and other lightweight alternatives pose competitive threats to steel in various applications, particularly in automotive and aerospace sectors. 3. Economic Fluctuations: Global economic downturns can lead to reduced demand for steel in key sectors such as construction and manufacturing. 4. Trade Policies and Tariffs: International trade tensions and protectionist policies can disrupt supply chains and affect export markets, impacting profitability.

Road Ahead

The Road Ahead for Aluminium manufacturing:

1. Green Aluminium: Demand for low-carbon aluminium is set to rise, driven by environmentally-conscious consumers and industries.

2. Advanced Applications: Aerospace, defense, and high-speed rail are just a few sectors where advanced aluminium applications will be in demand.

3. Integration with Technology: Incorporating AI, IoT, and machine learning can optimize production, reduce costs, and improve quality.

The Road Ahead for Steel Manufacturing:

1. Green Steel: The demand for low-carbon steel is expected to grow significantly as consumers and industries become more environmentally conscious. Initiatives such as using hydrogen-based reduction methods and electric arc furnaces, as well as increasing the use of scrap steel, will play a crucial role in reducing the carbon footprint of steel manufacturing. These efforts will not only align with stricter environmental regulations but also meet the rising demand for sustainable materials.

2. Advanced Applications: The steel industry will see increased demand in advanced applications across various sectors. High-strength and lightweight steel alloys will become essential in the automotive industry, especially for electric vehicles (EVs) that require materials to balance performance and energy efficiency. Additionally, sectors like renewable energy, particularly in wind turbines and solar panel mounts, as well as construction, aerospace, and defense, will require specialized steel products to meet specific technical and performance criteria.

3. Integration with Technology: Incorporating cutting-edge technologies such as Artificial Intelligence (AI), the Internet of Things (IoT), and machine learning will be pivotal in optimizing steel production. These technologies can enhance predictive maintenance, improve supply chain management, and ensure higher quality control. By adopting Industry 4.0 solutions, steel manufacturers can reduce operational costs, increase efficiency, and maintain a competitive edge in the global market. Enhanced data analytics will also facilitate better decision-making and innovation in product development.

The Aluminium Value Chain

Understanding the Aluminium value chain is crucial for potential investors and entrepreneurs looking to penetrate the market.

1. Bauxite Mining: This is the beginning, where raw bauxite ore is extracted from the earth.

2. Alumina Refining: The bauxite ore is processed to produce alumina, a white powder.

3. Primary Aluminium Production: Alumina is transformed into raw aluminium.

4. Downstream Aluminium Fabrication: The raw aluminium is then processed further into semi-finished or finished products.

5. Recycling: Used aluminium products are recycled back into the production cycle.

The Steel Value Chain

Understanding the steel value chain is essential for potential investors and entrepreneurs aiming to enter the market. Here are the key stages of the steel manufacturing process:

INDUSTRY 4.0 REVOLUTION

1. Iron Ore Mining: This is the initial stage where raw iron ore is extracted from the earth through mining. Iron ore is the primary raw material used in steel production.

2. Beneficiation and Pelletizing: The extracted iron ore undergoes beneficiation to improve its purity, removing impurities such as silica, phosphorous, and sulfur. The refined ore is then formed into pellets or sinter, making it suitable for the blast furnace.

3. Primary Steel Production: The next stage involves transforming the refined iron ore into crude steel. This can be done using various methods:

    * _Blast Furnace Method_: Iron ore, coke, and limestone are heated in a blast furnace to produce molten iron, which is then converted to steel in a basic oxygen furnace (BOF).

    * _Electric Arc Furnace (EAF) Method_: Scrap steel is melted using electric arcs, which is more energy-efficient and allows for higher recycling rates.

4. Secondary Steelmaking: In this phase, crude steel is refined and alloyed to achieve the desired chemical composition and mechanical properties. This involves processes like degassing, desulfurization, and adding alloying elements.

5. Casting and Hot Rolling: The molten steel is cast into semi-finished products such as slabs, billets, or blooms. These semi-finished products are then hot-rolled into various shapes like sheets, plates, bars, and structural sections.

6. Downstream Steel Fabrication: The hot-rolled products are further processed through cold rolling, coating, and other finishing processes to produce finished steel products such as pipes, wires, automotive parts, and construction materials.

7. Recycling: Steel is highly recyclable, and scrap steel from end-of-life products or manufacturing processes is collected and re-

melted in electric arc furnaces. Recycling plays a crucial role in the steel value chain, reducing the need for raw materials and energy.

By understanding the steel value chain, stakeholders can identify opportunities for investment and innovation, driving efficiency and sustainability in the steel industry.

Role of Technology in Aluminium Production

1. **Automation:** Modern factories rely heavily on automation for precision, repeatability, and efficiency.

2. **Data Analytics:** Predictive analytics can forecast demand, production glitches, and even maintenance requirements.

3. **Blockchain:** This technology can ensure the traceability of aluminium, proving its sustainability or origin.

4. **Artificial Intelligence:** AI can optimize supply chains, production schedules, and even improve safety.

Role of Technology in Steel Manufacturing

Technology plays a crucial role in modern steel manufacturing, driving innovation, efficiency, and sustainability across the entire production process.

1. **Automation:** Just like in aluminium production, modern steel factories heavily rely on automation for precision, repeatability, and efficiency. Automated systems control various stages of production, including raw material handling, melting, refining, casting, rolling, and finishing. Robotics and robotic arms are utilized for tasks such as material handling, welding, and quality control, leading to improved productivity, safety, and cost-effectiveness.

2. **Data Analytics:** Data analytics, including predictive analytics, play a vital role in optimizing steel production processes. Advanced

analytics algorithms analyze vast amounts of data from sensors, machines, and production systems to forecast demand, detect production glitches, and predict maintenance requirements. By leveraging data insights, steel manufacturers can optimize production schedules, reduce downtime, minimize waste, and enhance overall operational efficiency.

3. Blockchain: Similar to aluminium production, blockchain technology can be employed in the steel industry to ensure traceability and transparency throughout the supply chain. By recording and securely storing transactional data in a decentralized ledger, blockchain enables stakeholders to verify the authenticity and origin of steel products. This technology can prove the sustainability of steel production practices, track material provenance, and facilitate compliance with regulatory requirements and industry standards.

4. Artificial Intelligence: Artificial Intelligence (AI) holds immense potential for optimizing various aspects of steel manufacturing. AI algorithms can analyze complex data sets to optimize supply chains, production schedules, and inventory management. Machine learning algorithms can predict equipment failures and maintenance needs, allowing proactive maintenance and minimizing unplanned downtime. AI-powered systems can also improve safety by detecting and mitigating potential hazards in real-time, enhancing workplace safety for employees.

Thus, we can say, technology, including automation, data analytics, blockchain, and artificial intelligence, plays a transformative role in modern steel manufacturing, driving efficiency, sustainability, and competitiveness in the industry. Embracing and integrating these technologies into steel production processes will be essential for steel manufacturers to thrive in an increasingly digital and interconnected world.

In the book, Industry 4.0 and Startup represents a transformative force that is reshaping the manufacturing industry as we know it. By embracing digital technologies, automation, and data-driven insights, manufacturers can unlock new levels of efficiency, productivity, and innovation, positioning themselves for success in the digital age.

UNDERSTANDING DIGITAL TRANSFORMATION

Understanding Digital Transformation in Manufacturing: Unravel the concept of digital transformation and its profound impact on manufacturing processes. Discover the drivers and enablers of digital transformation, and gain insights into its transformative effects on operations.

- *Concept of Digital Transformation*
- *Drivers and Enablers of Digital Transformation*
- *Impact on Manufacturing Processes and Operations*

In today's fast-paced and interconnected world, digital transformation has emerged as a key imperative for manufacturers seeking to thrive in the Fourth Industrial Revolution. This chapter delves into the concept of digital transformation, explores its drivers and enablers, and examines its profound impact on manufacturing processes and operations. Despite the ongoing digital revolution in many industries, it has been relatively slow to adopt new technologies in heavy metal industries. However, it's important to note that implementing technology-based platforms doesn't mean replacing human workers.

Rather, it's a step towards increased efficiency and productivity. As business owners in the metal industry, it is crucial to embrace digitization and leverage the tools available to them. This includes not only the use of digitized technology but also the need for cybersecurity measures to protect against potential threats. While the adoption of new technologies in metal industries like Aluminium and Steel, may come with some challenges, the benefits it brings to the industry are well worth the effort.

Concept of Digital Transformation

Digital transformation can be defined as the strategic adoption and integration of digital technologies to fundamentally change business processes, models, and customer experiences. In the context of manufacturing, digital transformation entails the digitization of traditional processes and the adoption of advanced technologies to drive innovation, efficiency, and competitiveness.

At its core, digital transformation involves leveraging technologies such as IoT, artificial intelligence (AI), cloud computing, big data analytics, and robotics to create connected, data-driven ecosystems that enable smarter decision-making and more agile operations. It goes beyond simply automating existing processes to reimagine entire value chains and business models, driving new levels of productivity, flexibility, and customer satisfaction.

Drivers and Enablers of Digital Transformation

Several factors drive and enable digital transformation in manufacturing:

- *Technological Advancements*: The rapid evolution and convergence of digital technologies have made advanced solutions more accessible and affordable for manufacturers. Breakthroughs in areas such as IoT sensors, AI algorithms, and cloud computing have paved the way for transformative capabilities that were previously unimaginable.

- *Changing Customer Expectations*: In an era of personalized experiences and instant gratification, customers expect products to be tailored to their unique needs and delivered with speed and efficiency. Digital transformation enables manufacturers to meet these expectations by offering customizable products, faster turnaround times, sustainable and seamless omnichannel experiences.

- *Competitive Pressures*: Globalization and increasing competition have intensified pressure on manufacturers to differentiate themselves and operate more efficiently. Digital transformation provides a means to gain a competitive edge by optimizing processes, reducing costs, and delivering superior products and services.

- *Data Deluge*: The proliferation of data from various sources, including sensors, machines, and customer interactions, presents both a challenge and an opportunity for manufacturers. Digital transformation enables organizations to harness the power of big data analytics to extract actionable insights, drive informed decision-making, and unlock new business opportunities.

- *Regulatory Requirements*: Regulatory mandates and industry standards often require manufacturers to adhere to stringent quality, safety, and environmental regulations. Digital transformation can help organizations ensure compliance by implementing robust monitoring, reporting, and traceability systems.

- *Cultural Shift*: Embracing digital transformation requires a cultural shift within organizations, with a focus on fostering innovation, collaboration, and continuous learning. Leaders must champion a digital-first mindset and empower employees to embrace change, experiment with new technologies, and drive digital initiatives forward.

Impact on Manufacturing Processes and Operations

The adoption of digital transformation initiatives has a profound impact on various aspects of manufacturing processes and operations:

- *Streamlined Operations*: Digital transformation streamlines manufacturing operations by automating repetitive tasks, optimizing workflows, and eliminating manual inefficiencies. IoT-enabled sensors monitor equipment performance in real-time, enabling predictive maintenance and reducing downtime.

- *Enhanced Visibility and Control*: Digital technologies provide manufacturers with unprecedented visibility into their operations, supply chains, and customer interactions. Advanced analytics and AI algorithms analyze vast amounts of data to identify patterns, trends, and anomalies, enabling proactive decision-making and risk mitigation.

- *Agile Production*: Digital transformation enables manufacturers to respond quickly to changing market demands and customer preferences. Flexible manufacturing systems, powered by robotics and automation, allow for rapid reconfiguration and customization of production lines to accommodate varying product specifications and volumes.

- *Improved Quality and Compliance*: By integrating quality management systems with digital technologies, manufacturers can ensure adherence to stringent quality standards and regulatory requirements. Real-time monitoring and data analytics enable early detection of defects and deviations, minimizing rework and waste.

- *Empowered Workforce*: Digital transformation empowers employees with tools and technologies that enhance productivity, collaboration, and creativity. Augmented reality (AR) and virtual reality (VR) applications provide immersive training experiences, while digital workstations and mobile apps enable real-time communication and access to information.

- *Optimized Supply Chain*: Digital transformation extends beyond the factory floor to encompass the entire supply chain, from raw material sourcing to product delivery. Cloud-based platforms, blockchain technology, and IoT-enabled tracking systems enhance visibility, traceability, and collaboration across the supply chain network.

To wrap-up the chapter, digital transformation is revolutionizing the manufacturing industry by reshaping processes, driving innovation, and unlocking new value propositions. By embracing digital technologies and embracing a culture of continuous improvement, manufacturers can position themselves for success in an increasingly digital and interconnected world.

EMBRACING AUTOMATION AND ROBOTICS

Embracing Automation and Robotics: Explore the pivotal role of automation and robotics in modern manufacturing. Delve into different types of robotic applications, weigh their benefits against challenges, and understand how they revolutionize production.

- *Role of Automation and Robotics in Manufacturing*
- *Types of Robotic Applications*
- *Benefits and Challenges of Automation*

INDUSTRY 4.0 REVOLUTION

Revolutionizing Production Processes

Automation and robotics have become integral components of modern manufacturing, offering unparalleled efficiency, precision, and flexibility. This chapter explores the role of automation and robotics in manufacturing, examines various types of robotic applications, and discusses the benefits and challenges associated with their implementation.

Role of Automation and Robotics in Manufacturing

Automation and robotics play a critical role in revolutionizing manufacturing processes by streamlining operations, improving productivity, and enhancing quality. These technologies enable manufacturers to achieve higher levels of efficiency, accuracy, and consistency compared to traditional manual methods.

- *Streamlined Operations*: The metal industry has long relied on robotics for hazardous tasks, but traditional robots were bulky and required dedicated spaces. With advancements, collaborative robots (cobots) have emerged, working alongside humans for safer operations. Cobots excel in risky or repetitive tasks, easing labor shortages worsened by the pandemic. While still nascent in metal industries, cobots show promise, enhancing efficiency, cutting costs, and boosting precision. Automation and robotics reducing reliance on manual labor and minimizing human error. This leads to streamlined operations, shorter cycle times, and increased throughput, ultimately driving higher levels of productivity and profitability.

- *Improved Quality*: Robotics and automation systems offer unparalleled precision and repeatability, resulting in consistently high-quality products. By minimizing variations and defects, manufacturers can enhance customer satisfaction, reduce rework and waste, and maintain a competitive edge in the market.

- *Flexibility and Adaptability*: Modern robotics systems are highly flexible and adaptable, capable of performing a wide range of tasks and accommodating changes in production requirements. This flexibility enables manufacturers to respond quickly to shifting market demands, product variations, and customization requests.

- *Enhanced Safety*: Automation and robotics help create safer working environments by reducing exposure to hazardous conditions and repetitive strain injuries. Robots can handle tasks that are dangerous or ergonomically challenging for humans, minimizing the risk of workplace accidents and injuries.

- *Cost Savings*: While the initial investment in automation and robotics may be significant, the long-term cost savings can be substantial. These technologies reduce labor costs, improve resource utilization, and optimize energy consumption, leading to improved efficiency and profitability over time.

- *Competitive Advantage*: Manufacturers that embrace automation and robotics gain a competitive advantage by increasing their production capacity, reducing time-to-market, and delivering superior products at lower costs. This allows them to capture market share, expand their customer base, and outperform their competitors.

Types of Robotic Applications

Robotic applications in manufacturing span a wide range of industries, processes, and functions, including:

- *Material Handling*: Robots are widely used for material handling tasks such as loading, unloading, sorting, and palletizing. These robots can handle heavy payloads, operate in confined spaces, and perform repetitive tasks with speed and precision.

- *Assembly and Disassembly*: Robotics systems excel at assembling complex products with multiple components, such as electronics, automotive parts, and consumer goods. They can accurately position and manipulate parts, apply adhesives, and perform delicate assembly tasks with high dexterity.

- *Welding and Fabrication*: Industrial robots are commonly employed for welding, cutting, and fabrication tasks in industries such as automotive, aerospace, and metalworking. These robots offer high repeatability, consistent weld quality, and increased throughput compared to manual welding processes.

- *Painting and Coating*: Painting and coating applications require precision and uniformity to achieve desired surface finishes and coatings. Robots equipped with spray guns or applicators can apply paints, adhesives, sealants, and coatings with precision and consistency, reducing waste and improving quality.

- *Inspection and Quality Control*: Robots equipped with sensors, cameras, and vision systems can perform inspection and quality control tasks with speed and accuracy. These robots can identify defects, measure dimensions, and verify product integrity, ensuring compliance with quality standards and specifications.

- *Packaging and Palletizing*: Robotic packaging systems automate the packaging process by picking, placing, and palletizing products into containers or shipping cartons. These robots can handle a wide range of products, sizes, and shapes, maximizing efficiency and throughput in packaging operations.

Benefits and Challenges of Automation

While automation and robotics offer numerous benefits, they also present certain challenges and considerations for manufacturers:

- *Initial Investment*: The upfront cost of implementing automation and robotics systems can be substantial, including equipment, software, integration, and training expenses. Manufacturers must carefully evaluate the return on investment (ROI) and total cost of ownership (TCO) to justify the investment.

- *Integration Complexity*: Integrating robotics and automation systems into existing production lines and workflows can be complex and time-consuming. Manufacturers must ensure compatibility with existing equipment, software, and processes while minimizing disruption to operations.

- *Skill Requirements*: Operating and maintaining robotics systems requires specialized skills and expertise, including programming, troubleshooting, and preventive maintenance. Manufacturers may need to invest in training programs or recruit qualified personnel to operate and support these systems effectively.

- *Safety Concerns*: While robots can improve workplace safety by reducing exposure to hazardous conditions, they also introduce new safety risks, such as collisions, entrapment, and pinch points. Manufacturers must implement appropriate safety measures, such as barriers, sensors, and safety protocols, to protect workers and equipment.

- *Flexibility and Scalability*: Achieving flexibility and scalability in automation systems can be challenging, especially in dynamic or rapidly changing environments. Manufacturers must design systems that can adapt to evolving production requirements, product variations.

LEVERAGING IOT AND PREDICTIVE ANALYTICS

Leveraging IoT and Predictive Analytics: Step into the world of the Internet of Things (IoT) and predictive analytics, where data-driven decisions reign supreme. Learn how IoT applications optimize manufacturing processes and how predictive analytics ensures proactive maintenance and optimization.

- *Introduction to Internet of Things (IoT)*
- *Applications of IoT in Manufacturing*
- *Predictive Analytics for Maintenance and Optimization*

Transforming Operations with Data-Driven Insights

The integration of Internet of Things (IoT) devices and predictive analytics has revolutionized the manufacturing industry, enabling organizations to gather real-time data, optimize processes, and predict maintenance needs with unprecedented accuracy. In this chapter, we explore the fundamentals of IoT, examine its applications in manufacturing, and delve into the power of predictive analytics for maintenance and optimization.

Introduction to Internet of Things (IoT)

The Internet of Things (IoT) refers to a network of interconnected devices, sensors, and objects that collect and exchange data over the internet. These devices, often equipped with sensors and actuators, enable real-time monitoring, control, and automation of physical processes and environments. In the manufacturing context, IoT devices are deployed throughout the production facility to gather data on equipment performance, energy consumption, environmental conditions, and product quality.

- *IoT Architecture*: IoT systems typically consist of three main components: sensors and actuators, connectivity infrastructure, and data processing and analytics platforms. Sensors capture data from the physical environment, while actuators enable remote control and automation. Connectivity infrastructure, such as wireless networks or cloud platforms, facilitates data transmission and communication. Data processing and analytics platforms analyze the collected data to extract actionable insights and enable decision-making.

- *Key Features of IoT*: IoT devices offer several key features that make them well-suited for manufacturing applications, including:

- *Real-time Data Monitoring*: IoT devices continuously collect data from connected sensors, providing real-time insights into equipment performance, process parameters, and environmental conditions.

- *Remote Monitoring and Control*: Manufacturers can remotely monitor and control equipment and processes using IoT-enabled devices, reducing the need for on-site inspections and interventions.

- *Predictive Maintenance*: By analyzing historical and real-time data, IoT systems can predict equipment failures and maintenance needs, enabling proactive maintenance and minimizing downtime.

- *Energy Efficiency*: IoT devices can optimize energy usage by monitoring energy consumption, identifying inefficiencies, and implementing energy-saving measures.

- *Quality Assurance*: IoT-enabled sensors can monitor product quality parameters in real-time, enabling early detection of defects and deviations from specifications.

Applications of IoT in Manufacturing

IoT technology finds a wide range of applications in manufacturing, transforming various aspects of production, operations, and supply chain management. Some key applications include:

- *Condition Monitoring*: IoT sensors monitor equipment health and performance in real-time, detecting anomalies, deviations, and potential failures. This enables predictive maintenance strategies, reduces unplanned downtime, and extends equipment lifespan.

- *Asset Tracking and Management*: IoT-enabled tracking devices provide real-time visibility into the location, status, and usage of assets, such as raw materials, work-in-progress inventory, and finished goods. This improves inventory management, asset utilization, and supply chain efficiency.

- *Remote Diagnostics and Troubleshooting*: IoT devices enable remote diagnostics and troubleshooting of equipment issues, reducing the need for on-site inspections and service calls. Technicians can remotely access equipment data, diagnose problems, and implement corrective actions in real-time.

- *Energy Management*: IoT systems monitor energy consumption patterns, identify energy inefficiencies, and optimize energy usage across manufacturing facilities. This reduces energy costs, carbon emissions, and environmental impact while enhancing sustainability.

- *Quality Control*: IoT sensors monitor product quality parameters, such as dimensions, temperature, and humidity, throughout the production process. Any deviations from quality standards trigger alerts, enabling corrective actions to maintain product quality and compliance.

Predictive Analytics for Maintenance and Optimization

Predictive analytics leverages historical and real-time data to forecast future events, trends, and outcomes, enabling proactive decision-making and intervention. In the manufacturing context, predictive analytics is used primarily for maintenance and optimization purposes.

- *Predictive Maintenance*: Predictive analytics algorithms analyze equipment data to identify patterns, trends, and anomalies indicative of potential failures or maintenance needs. By predicting equipment failures before they occur, manufacturers can schedule preventive maintenance activities, minimize downtime, and avoid costly repairs.

- *Equipment Optimization*: Predictive analytics algorithms optimize equipment performance by identifying inefficiencies, bottlenecks, and optimization opportunities. By analyzing operational data, these algorithms recommend process improvements, parameter adjustments, and maintenance interventions to maximize throughput, quality, and efficiency.

- *Supply Chain Optimization*: Predictive analytics algorithms forecast demand, anticipate supply chain disruptions, and optimize inventory levels, distribution routes, and procurement strategies. By analyzing historical sales data, market trends, and external factors, these algorithms help manufacturers optimize their supply chain operations, reduce costs, and improve customer satisfaction.

- *Quality Prediction*: Predictive analytics algorithms predict product quality outcomes based on process parameters, raw material characteristics, and environmental conditions. By analyzing historical production data, these algorithms identify factors that influence product quality and recommend adjustments to production processes to minimize defects and ensure compliance with quality standards.

Conclusion

The combination of IoT technology and predictive analytics has transformed manufacturing operations, enabling organizations to achieve unprecedented levels of efficiency, reliability, and competitiveness. By leveraging real-time data insights, manufacturers can optimize equipment performance, improve product quality, and minimize downtime, ultimately driving operational excellence and business success. As IoT adoption continues to accelerate, the manufacturing industry is poised to reap the benefits of a data-driven future, ushering in a new era of innovation and productivity.

POWER OF DATA ANALYTICS

Harnessing the Power of Data Analytics: Unlock the potential of data analytics in manufacturing. Discover techniques for data collection and analysis, and understand how business intelligence derived from data drives strategic decision-making.

- *Importance of Data Analytics in Manufacturing*
- *Data Collection and Analysis Techniques*
- *Business Intelligence and Decision-Making*

Driving Innovation and Decision-Making

In the digital age, manufacturing organizations are inundated with vast amounts of data generated from various sources such as sensors, machines, and production processes. Harnessing this data and deriving actionable insight through data analytics has become imperative for driving innovation, improving efficiency, and making informed decisions. In this chapter, we explore the importance of data analytics in manufacturing, delve into data collection and analysis techniques, and examine how business intelligence facilitates effective decision-making.

Importance of Data Analytics in Manufacturing

Data analytics plays a pivotal role in manufacturing by enabling organizations to extract valuable insights from data, identify patterns, trends, and anomalies, and make data-driven decisions. Some key reasons why data analytics is crucial in manufacturing include:

- *Optimizing Operations*: Data analytics allows manufacturers to monitor and analyze key performance indicators (KPIs) in real-time, identify inefficiencies, and optimize production processes. By understanding production bottlenecks, resource utilization, and cycle times, manufacturers can streamline operations, increase throughput, and reduce costs.

- *Improving Quality Control*: Data analytics enables manufacturers to monitor product quality parameters, detect defects, and identify root causes of quality issues. By analyzing production data, manufacturers can implement corrective actions, improve process control, and enhance product quality and consistency.

- *Predictive Maintenance*: Data analytics algorithms analyze equipment data to predict potential equipment failures and maintenance needs. By monitoring equipment health, performance, and usage patterns, manufacturers can schedule preventive maintenance activities, minimize downtime, and avoid costly repairs.

- *Supply Chain Optimization*: Data analytics provides insights into supply chain dynamics, demand patterns, and inventory levels. By analyzing supply chain data, manufacturers can optimize inventory levels, reduce lead times, and improve delivery performance, ultimately enhancing customer satisfaction and loyalty.

- *Enabling Innovation*: Data analytics fosters innovation by providing insights into market trends, customer preferences, and emerging technologies. By analyzing market data and consumer feedback, manufacturers can identify new product opportunities, develop innovative solutions, and stay ahead of the competition.

Data Collection and Analysis Techniques

Effective data analytics in manufacturing relies on robust data collection and analysis techniques. Some common techniques used for data collection and analysis includes:

- *Data Collection*: Manufacturers collect data from various sources such as sensors, machines, production systems, and enterprise systems. Data can be collected in real-time or batch mode, depending on the application requirements. Common data collection methods include manual data entry, automated data logging, and sensor-based data acquisition.

- *Data Preprocessing*: Before analysis, raw data often undergoes preprocessing to clean, transform, and format it for analysis. Preprocessing steps may include data cleaning to remove outliers and errors, data normalization to scale data to a common range, and feature extraction to identify relevant variables for analysis.

- *Descriptive Analytics*: Descriptive analytics involves summarizing and visualizing data to gain insights into historical trends and patterns. Common descriptive analytics techniques include statistical analysis, data visualization, and exploratory data analysis (EDA). Descriptive analytics helps manufacturers understand past performance and identify areas for improvement.

- *Predictive Analytics*: Predictive analytics uses statistical algorithms and machine learning techniques to forecast future outcomes based on historical and real-time data. Predictive analytics models can predict equipment failures, demand trends, and market fluctuations, enabling proactive decision-making and intervention.

- *Prescriptive Analytics*: Prescriptive analytics goes beyond prediction to recommend optimal courses of action based on predictive insights. Prescriptive analytics models identify the best strategies for achieving specific business objectives, such as minimizing costs, maximizing efficiency, or optimizing resource allocation.

Business Intelligence and Decision-Making

Business intelligence (BI) refers to the use of data analytics tools and techniques to transform raw data into actionable insights for decision-making. In manufacturing, BI enables organizations to monitor performance, analyze trends, and make informed decisions at various levels of the organization. Some key aspects of BI in manufacturing include:

- *Performance Monitoring*: BI dashboards and scorecards provide real-time visibility into key performance indicators (KPIs) such as production output, quality metrics, and equipment downtime. By monitoring KPIs, managers can identify areas of concern, track progress towards goals, and take corrective actions as needed.

- *Root Cause Analysis*: BI tools facilitate root cause analysis by correlating data from multiple sources to identify underlying factors contributing to performance issues or quality defects. By drilling down into data, managers can uncover root causes, implement corrective actions, and prevent recurrence of problems.

- *Trend Analysis*: BI enables trend analysis by analyzing historical data to identify patterns, trends, and anomalies over time. By analyzing trends, managers can identify emerging opportunities, anticipate market shifts, and make strategic decisions to capitalize on changing market dynamics.

- *Predictive Insights*: BI tools can integrate predictive analytics models to provide actionable insights for predictive maintenance, demand forecasting, and inventory optimization. By leveraging predictive insights, managers can anticipate future events, mitigate risks, and optimize resource allocation for better decision-making.

- *Data Visualization*: BI platforms offer data visualization capabilities, allowing users to create interactive charts, graphs, and other visual representations of data. These tools enable users to explore and analyze data in a more intuitive and user-friendly manner, facilitating better understanding and interpretation of complex datasets.

Additionally, data visualization helps users communicate insights effectively to stakeholders, driving informed decision-making and driving business value.

SUPPLY CHAIN OPTIMIZATION

Supply Chain Optimization in the Digital Age: Explore the evolution of supply chain management and the challenges faced by traditional supply chains. Discover digital solutions that optimize supply chain operations and enhance efficiency in the digital age.

- *Overview of Supply Chain Management.*
- *Challenges in Traditional Supply Chains.*
- *Digital Solutions for Supply Chain Optimization.*

Transforming Traditional Practices

In the digital age, supply chain optimization has become a critical imperative for manufacturing organizations seeking to enhance efficiency, reduce costs, and improve customer satisfaction. This chapter explores the evolution of supply chain management, the challenges faced by traditional supply chains, and the digital solutions that are revolutionizing supply chain optimization.

Overview of Supply Chain Management

Supply chain management (SCM) encompasses the planning, procurement, production, and distribution of goods and services from suppliers to end customers. Traditionally, supply chain management involved linear, sequential processes with limited visibility and coordination across the supply chain. However, with the advent of globalization, increasing customer expectations, and rapid technological advancements, supply chain management has evolved into a complex, interconnected ecosystem.

Modern supply chains are characterized by global sourcing, outsourcing, and distributed manufacturing networks, making them more susceptible to disruptions and uncertainties. Effective supply chain management requires collaboration, visibility, and agility to respond to dynamic market conditions and customer demands.

Challenges in Traditional Supply Chains

Traditional supply chains face several challenges that impede efficiency, responsiveness, and profitability. Some common challenges include:

- *Limited Visibility*: Traditional supply chains lack end-to-end visibility, making it difficult to track inventory, monitor supplier performance, and anticipate disruptions. Lack of visibility leads to inefficiencies, excess inventory, and increased operating costs.

- *Fragmented Processes*: Traditional supply chains are characterized by fragmented, siloed processes with limited coordination and collaboration across functional areas. This fragmentation results in inefficiencies, redundancies, and delays in decision-making and execution.

- *Inventory Management*: In traditional supply chains, inventory management is often based on forecasted demand rather than real-time data. This leads to overstocking, stockouts, and excess carrying costs, impacting profitability and customer service levels.

- *Supply Chain Risks*: Traditional supply chains are susceptible to various risks such as supplier disruptions, geopolitical instability, natural disasters, and cybersecurity threats. Failure to mitigate these risks can result in supply chain disruptions, production delays, and reputational damage.

- *Customer Expectations*: With the rise of e-commerce and omnichannel retailing, customer expectations for speed, flexibility, and personalization have increased. Traditional supply chains struggle to meet these evolving customer demands, leading to dissatisfaction and churn.

Digital Solutions for Supply Chain Optimization

To address the challenges faced by traditional supply chains, manufacturers are turning to digital solutions that leverage advanced technologies to enhance visibility, agility, and efficiency. Some key digital solutions for supply chain optimization include:

- *Supply Chain Visibility Platforms*: Digital supply chain visibility platforms provide real-time insights into inventory levels, supplier performance, transportation status, and order fulfillment. By aggregating data from multiple sources, these platforms enable organizations to track shipments, identify bottlenecks, and proactively manage exceptions.

- *Predictive Analytics*: Predictive analytics uses historical data, machine learning algorithms, and statistical models to forecast demand, optimize inventory levels, and mitigate supply chain risks. By analyzing patterns and trends, predictive analytics helps organizations anticipate future demand fluctuations and optimize inventory replenishment strategies.

- *Blockchain Technology*: Blockchain technology offers a secure, transparent, and immutable ledger for tracking and tracing goods throughout the supply chain. By creating a decentralized database of transactions, blockchain enables end-to-end visibility, authenticity verification, and tamper-proof record-keeping. Blockchain enhances supply chain transparency, reduces counterfeiting, and improves trust and collaboration among supply chain partners.

- *Internet of Things (IoT)*: The Internet of Things (IoT) connects physical objects such as sensors, devices, and machinery to the internet, enabling real-time monitoring and control of supply chain assets. IoT sensors collect data on temperature, humidity, location, and condition, providing organizations with visibility into supply chain operations and asset performance. IoT enables proactive maintenance, asset tracking, and condition monitoring, reducing downtime and improving asset utilization.

- *Artificial Intelligence (AI)*: Artificial intelligence (AI) algorithms analyze vast amounts of supply chain data to identify patterns, optimize routes, and predict potential disruptions. AI-powered forecasting models improve demand planning accuracy, while AI-driven optimization algorithms optimize inventory allocation, production scheduling, and transportation routing. AI enhances decision-making, reduces costs, and improves operational efficiency across the supply chain.

Conclusion

In conclusion, supply chain optimization is critical for manufacturers seeking to remain competitive in today's fast-paced, global marketplace. By embracing digital solutions such as supply chain visibility platforms, predictive analytics, blockchain technology, IoT, and AI, organizations can enhance visibility, agility, and efficiency in their supply chains. By addressing the challenges faced by traditional supply chains and leveraging digital technologies, manufacturers can streamline operations, reduce costs, and deliver superior customer experiences.

DIGITAL TWIN TECHNOLOGY EXPLORATION

Exploring Digital Twin Technology: Enter the realm of digital twin technology, where virtual replicas transform manufacturing. Learn about its components, applications, and the promising future it holds for the industry.

- Concept and Components of Digital Twin.
- Applications in Manufacturing.
- Benefits and Future Prospects.

INDUSTRY 4.0 REVOLUTION

A Revolution in Manufacturing

Digital twin technology represents a paradigm shift in the manufacturing industry, offering unprecedented opportunities for innovation, optimization, and efficiency. In this chapter, we delve into the concept and components of digital twin technology, explore its diverse applications in manufacturing, and examine the myriad benefits and future prospects it holds for the industry.

Concept and Components of Digital Twin

At its core, a digital twin is a virtual representation of a physical object, process, or system that mirrors its real-world counterpart in a digital environment. Digital twins are created using a combination of technologies such as sensors, IoT devices, cloud computing, and data analytics to capture, simulate, and analyze real-time data from physical assets.

The components of a digital twin typically include:

- *Physical Asset*: The physical asset or system that is being digitized, such as a machine, production line, or entire manufacturing industry.

- *Virtual Model*: A digital replica or model of the physical asset, comprising geometric, functional, and behavioral characteristics.

- *Data Integration Layer*: The data integration layer connects the physical asset to its digital twin, facilitating the exchange of data between the two environments.

- *Sensor and IoT Infrastructure*: Sensors and IoT devices embedded within the physical asset collect real-time data on parameters such as temperature, pressure, vibration, and energy consumption.

- *Cloud-Based Analytics Platform*: A cloud-based analytics platform processes and analyzes the data collected from the physical asset, generating insights, predictions, and recommendations.

- *Visualization and User Interface*: Visualization tools and user interfaces enable users to interact with the digital twin, visualize data, and perform simulations and analyses.

By integrating these components, digital twin technology enables manufacturers to create dynamic, data-driven representations of their assets and processes, facilitating real-time monitoring, analysis, and optimization.

Applications in Manufacturing

Digital twin technology finds myriad applications across various stages of the manufacturing lifecycle, from product design and development to production, maintenance, and optimization. Some key applications include:

- *Product Design and Prototyping*: Digital twins enable industries to create virtual prototypes of products, simulate their performance under different conditions, and optimize design parameters before physical prototypes are built. This reduces time-to-market, minimizes design iterations, and improves product quality.

- *Production Planning and Simulation*: Digital twins of manufacturing facilities allow planners to simulate production processes, optimize production & maintenance schedules, and identify potential bottlenecks or inefficiencies. By simulating "what-if" scenarios, manufacturers can anticipate and mitigate risks, improve resource utilization, and optimize production throughput.

- *Predictive Maintenance*: Digital twins of equipment and machinery enable predictive maintenance strategies, allowing manufacturers to monitor asset health in real-time, predict potential failures, and schedule maintenance proactively. By identifying maintenance needs before they escalate into costly breakdowns, manufacturers can minimize downtime, reduce maintenance costs, and extend asset lifespan.

- *Quality Control and Process Optimization*: Digital twins facilitate real-time monitoring and analysis of manufacturing processes, enabling manufacturers to identify deviations, anomalies, or defects and take corrective actions in real-time. By optimizing process parameters, manufacturers can improve product quality in a close loop, reduce scrap and rework, and enhance overall process efficiency.

- *Supply Chain Management*: Digital twins of supply chain networks provide end-to-end visibility into inventory levels, transportation routes, and production schedules, enabling manufacturers to optimize inventory management, minimize stockouts, and improve supply chain responsiveness in a digital environment without calling manual intervenes. By integrating digital twins across the supply chain, manufacturers can achieve greater coordination, collaboration, and efficiency.

Benefits and Future Prospects

The adoption of digital twin technology offers manufacturers a wide range of benefits, including:

- *Improved Operational Efficiency*: Digital twins enable real-time monitoring, analysis, and optimization of manufacturing processes, leading to improved efficiency, productivity, and resource utilization.

- *Reduced Downtime and Maintenance Costs*: Predictive maintenance enabled by digital twins minimizes unplanned downtime, reduces maintenance costs, and extends asset lifespan through proactive maintenance strategies.

- *Enhanced Product Quality*: Digital twins facilitate real-time quality monitoring and control, enabling manufacturers to detect defects, anomalies, or deviations early in the production process and take corrective actions to ensure template product quality.

- *Accelerated Innovation and Time-to-Market*: By enabling virtual prototyping, simulation, and optimization, digital twins accelerate the innovation cycle, reduce time-to-market, and enable manufacturers to bring new products to market faster.

- *Optimized Supply Chain Management*: Digital twins of supply chain networks provide end-to-end visibility and enable proactive decision-making, leading to optimized inventory management, reduced stockouts, and improved supply chain responsiveness.

Looking ahead, the future prospects of digital twin technology in manufacturing are promising. Advances in AI algorithm, machine learning, and edge computing will further enhance the capabilities of digital twins, enabling more sophisticated simulations, predictive analytics, and autonomous real time decision-making. Additionally, the integration of digital twins across the entire manufacturing ecosystem, from design and production to supply chain and service, will drive greater collaboration, efficiency, and innovation in the metal manufacturing industries.

In conclusion, digital twin technology represents a transformative force in the manufacturing industry, offering unparalleled opportunities for optimization, innovation, and competitiveness. By embracing digital transformation and harnessing the power of digital twins, manufacturers, especially in the metal manufacturing sector, can streamline operations and enhance productivity. This adoption ensures they stay ahead of the curve in an increasingly digitalized and innovative global business world, fostering a robust startup ecosystem and thriving in a competitive landscape. As we navigate this revolutionary era, the symbiotic relationship between traditional manufacturing practices and cutting-edge technology paves the way for a future where efficiency, sustainability, and growth are harmoniously intertwined.

Let's explore the impact of digital twins on manufacturing and uncover future opportunities. Together, we can shape a future defined by digital transformation, innovation, and sustainable growth, ensuring lasting progress for future generations.

CLOUD COMPUTING: THE GAME CHANGER

Cloud Computing for Manufacturing Excellence: Embark on a journey into the cloud, where manufacturing operations are revolutionized. Understand the fundamentals of cloud computing, its deployment models, and its myriad applications in manufacturing.

- *Introduction to Cloud Computing.*
- *Cloud Deployment Models.*
- *Cloud Applications in Manufacturing.*

Cloud computing has emerged as a game-changer in the manufacturing industry, revolutionizing how businesses operate, collaborate, and innovate. This chapter provides an in-depth exploration of cloud computing, including its fundamental concepts, deployment models, and various applications in manufacturing.

Introduction to Cloud Computing

Cloud computing refers to the delivery of computing services—including servers, storage, databases, networking, software, and analytics—over the internet, offering on-demand access to shared computing resources. Unlike traditional on-premises IT infrastructure, where companies manage their own servers and software, cloud computing allows organizations to access computing resources hosted by third-party providers on a pay-as-you-go basis. This shift from traditional IT models to cloud-based solutions offers numerous benefits, including scalability, flexibility, cost-efficiency, and enhanced agility.

Cloud Deployment Models

There are several deployment models for cloud computing, each offering different levels of control, security, and customization options:

- *Public Cloud*: In a public cloud model, cloud services are provided over the public internet by third-party providers, such as Amazon Web Services (AWS), Microsoft Azure, and Google Cloud Platform (GCP). Public clouds are highly scalable and cost-effective, as customers only pay for the resources they use on a pay-per-use basis. However, public clouds may raise concerns about data security and compliance, as data is stored on shared infrastructure.

- *Private Cloud*: A private cloud is dedicated to a single organization and is hosted either on-premises or by a third-party provider. Private clouds offer greater control, security, and customization options compared to public clouds, making them ideal for organizations with stringent security and compliance requirements. However, private clouds may require higher upfront investment and ongoing maintenance costs.

- *Hybrid Cloud*: A hybrid cloud environment combines the benefits of both public and private clouds, allowing organizations to leverage the scalability and cost-efficiency of public clouds while maintaining control over sensitive data and applications in private clouds. Hybrid clouds offer flexibility and agility, enabling seamless integration between on-premises infrastructure and public cloud services.

- *Multi-Cloud*: A multi-cloud strategy involves using multiple cloud providers to avoid vendor lock-in, optimize costs, and leverage best-of-breed services from different providers. Multi-cloud environments enable organizations to distribute workloads across multiple clouds for redundancy, resilience, and performance optimization. However, managing multiple cloud environments may require additional resources and expertise.

Cloud Applications in Manufacturing

Cloud computing offers a wide range of applications and use cases in the manufacturing industry, enabling organizations to streamline operations, optimize processes, and drive innovation. Some common applications of cloud computing in manufacturing include:

- *Data Storage and Backup*: Cloud storage solutions allow manufacturers to securely store and back up large volumes of data, including product designs, manufacturing data, and operational records. Cloud storage offers scalability, accessibility, and reliability, ensuring that critical data is always available when needed.

- *Collaboration and Communication*: Cloud-based collaboration tools, such as document sharing platforms, project management software, and video conferencing solutions, facilitate real-time communication and collaboration among geographically dispersed teams. Cloud-based collaboration tools improve productivity, efficiency, and decision-making, enabling seamless collaboration across departments and locations.

- *Enterprise Resource Planning (ERP)*: Cloud-based ERP systems centralize and automate key business processes, including inventory management, production planning, supply chain management, and financial accounting. Cloud-based ERP solutions offer scalability, flexibility, and cost-efficiency, allowing manufacturers to adapt to changing business needs and market dynamics.

- *Product Lifecycle Management (PLM)*: Cloud-based PLM platforms enable manufacturers to manage the entire product lifecycle, from concept and design to manufacturing and service. Cloud-based PLM solutions facilitate collaboration among cross-functional teams, streamline design and engineering processes, and accelerate time-to-market for new products.

- *Internet of Things (IoT) Integration*: Cloud computing provides a scalable and flexible infrastructure for collecting, storing, and analyzing data from IoT devices deployed on the manufacturing shop floor. Cloud-based IoT platforms enable manufacturers to monitor equipment health, optimize production processes, and implement predictive maintenance strategies based on real-time data insights.

In conclusion, cloud computing holds tremendous potential to drive manufacturing excellence by providing scalable, flexible, and cost-effective solutions for data storage, collaboration, ERP, PLM, IoT integration, and more. By embracing cloud computing technologies, manufacturers can gain a competitive edge in today's digital economy and unlock new opportunities for innovation and growth.

BLOCKCHAIN REVOLUTIONIZES SUPPLY CHAIN

Blockchain Integration in Supply Chains: Delve into the world of blockchain technology and its transformative potential in supply chain management. Explore real-world applications, advantages, and the challenges of blockchain integration.

- *Understanding Blockchain Technology.*
- *Use Cases in Supply Chain Management.*
- *Advantages and Implementation Challenges.*

INDUSTRY 4.0 REVOLUTION

Blockchain technology has gained significant attention in recent years for its potential to revolutionize supply chain management by providing transparency, traceability, and security across the entire supply chain. In this chapter, we will explore the fundamentals of blockchain technology, its applications in supply chain management, and the advantages and implementation challenges associated with blockchain integration.

Understanding Blockchain Technology

Blockchain is a decentralized, distributed ledger technology that enables secure and transparent recording of transactions across multiple parties in a tamper-proof manner. At its core, a blockchain is a series of blocks containing transaction data, which are linked together in a chronological and immutable chain. Each block contains a cryptographic hash of the previous block, creating a secure and tamper-proof record of transactions.

Key features of blockchain technology include

- *Decentralization*: Unlike traditional centralized databases, blockchain operates on a decentralized network of computers (nodes), where each node stores a copy of the entire blockchain. This decentralized architecture ensures that no single entity has control over the data, making blockchain resistant to censorship and tampering.

- *Transparency*: Transactions recorded on the blockchain are visible to all participants in the network, providing transparency and accountability. Each participant can view the entire transaction history and verify the authenticity of transactions in real-time.

- *Immutability*: Once a transaction is recorded on the blockchain, it cannot be altered or deleted. Each block is linked to the previous block using cryptographic hashes, making it virtually impossible to tamper with past transactions without detection.

- *Security*: Blockchain employs cryptographic techniques such as digital signatures and consensus mechanisms to ensure the integrity and security of transactions. Transactions are verified and validated by the network participants through a consensus algorithm, ensuring that only valid transactions are added to the blockchain.

Use Cases in Supply Chain Management

Blockchain technology has numerous applications in supply chain management, enabling organizations to enhance transparency, traceability, and efficiency throughout the supply chain. Some common use cases of blockchain in supply chain management include:

- *Traceability*: Blockchain enables end-to-end traceability of products throughout the supply chain, from raw material sourcing to production, distribution, and delivery. Each transaction or movement of goods is recorded on the blockchain, allowing stakeholders to track the journey of products in real-time.

- *Provenance Tracking*: Blockchain can be used to authenticate the origin and authenticity of products by recording detailed information about their production, handling, and transportation on the blockchain. This helps to combat counterfeiting, fraud, and product recalls by providing verifiable proof of authenticity.

- *Inventory Management*: Blockchain facilitates real-time visibility and transparency of inventory levels and movements across multiple parties in the supply chain. By recording inventory transactions on the blockchain, organizations can optimize inventory management, reduce stockouts and excess inventory, and improve supply chain efficiency.

- *Supplier Management*: Blockchain enables secure and transparent management of supplier relationships by recording supplier information, contracts, and transactions on the blockchain. This helps to streamline supplier onboarding, monitor supplier performance, and ensure compliance with contractual agreements.

Advantages and Implementation Challenges

While blockchain technology offers numerous benefits for supply chain management, including enhanced transparency, traceability, and security, its implementation poses several challenges:

- *Scalability*: One of the main challenges of blockchain implementation is scalability, as the current generation of blockchain platforms may struggle to handle the high transaction volumes and processing speeds required by large-scale supply chain networks. Scalability solutions such as sharding, sidechains, and off-chain scaling are being explored to address this challenge.

- *Interoperability*: Ensuring interoperability between different blockchain platforms and legacy systems is another challenge, as supply chain networks often involve multiple stakeholders using different technologies and standards. Interoperability standards and protocols are needed to enable seamless data exchange and integration across disparate systems.

- *Data Privacy and Security*: While blockchain offers enhanced security through its cryptographic features, ensuring data privacy and security remains a concern, particularly in public blockchain networks where data is visible to all participants. Privacy-enhancing techniques such as zero-knowledge proofs and homomorphic encryption are being developed to address this challenge.

- *Regulatory Compliance*: Blockchain implementation in supply chain management may raise regulatory and legal concerns, particularly regarding data protection, intellectual property rights, and cross-border data transfer. Organizations must navigate complex regulatory frameworks and ensure compliance with applicable laws and regulations.

In conclusion, blockchain technology has the potential to transform supply chain management by providing transparency, traceability, and security across the entire supply chain. While blockchain offers numerous benefits for supply chain management, including enhanced transparency, traceability, and security, its implementation poses several challenges that must be addressed to unlock its full potential.

By understanding the fundamentals of blockchain technology, exploring its applications in supply chain management, and addressing implementation challenges, organizations can harness the power of blockchain to drive innovation and efficiency in their supply chains.

AR AND VR TECHNOLOGY

Augmented Reality and Virtual Reality Applications in Manufacturing: Immerse yourself in the world of AR and VR technologies, where reality is augmented and virtual. Discover their applications in training, maintenance, and design, and envision future trends.

- *Overview of AR and VR Technologies.*
- *Applications in Training, Maintenance, and Design.*
- *Future Trends and Developments.*

Augmented Reality (AR) and Virtual Reality (VR) technologies have gained significant traction in the manufacturing industry, offering innovative solutions to enhance training, maintenance, and design processes. In this chapter, we will provide an overview of AR and VR technologies, explore their applications in manufacturing, and discuss future trends and developments in this rapidly evolving field.

Overview of AR and VR Technologies

Augmented Reality (AR) and Virtual Reality (VR) are immersive technologies that overlay digital content onto the real world or create entirely virtual environments, respectively. While both AR and VR offer immersive experiences, they differ in their approach and applications.

Augmented Reality (AR) enhances the real world by overlaying digital information, such as images, videos, or 3D models, onto the user's view of the physical environment. AR applications can be accessed through smartphones, tablets, wearable devices, or specialized AR glasses, allowing users to interact with digital content in real-time while maintaining awareness of their surroundings.

Virtual Reality (VR), on the other hand, creates entirely immersive virtual environments that users can explore and interact with using VR headsets or goggles. VR technology transports users to virtual worlds, enabling them to experience simulations, training scenarios, or design prototypes in a fully immersive manner.

Applications in Training, Maintenance, and Design

AR and VR technologies offer a wide range of applications in manufacturing, including training, maintenance, and design:

- *Training*: AR and VR are transforming training processes by providing immersive and interactive learning experiences for employees. Manufacturers can use AR and VR simulations to train workers on equipment operation, assembly procedures, safety protocols, and troubleshooting techniques in a realistic virtual environment. This enables employees to gain hands-on experience and practical skills in a safe and controlled setting, reducing the need for traditional classroom-based training and minimizing the risk of accidents or errors on the shop floor.

- *Maintenance*: AR and VR technologies are revolutionizing maintenance processes by enabling technicians to access digital instructions, overlay information onto physical objects, and perform maintenance tasks more efficiently. AR-based maintenance applications can provide technicians with real-time diagnostic information, step-by-step repair instructions, and visual guidance overlaid onto the equipment or machinery they are servicing. This enhances troubleshooting capabilities, reduces downtime, and improves the overall efficiency of maintenance operations.

- *Design*: AR and VR technologies are reshaping the design process by enabling engineers and designers to visualize and prototype products in virtual environments. VR-based design tools allow designers to create and manipulate 3D models of products, components, or factory layouts in a virtual space, providing valuable insights into form, function, and ergonomics. AR applications can superimpose digital prototypes onto physical objects or environments, allowing designers to assess design concepts in real-world contexts and make informed decisions early in the design process.

Future Trends and Developments

The future of AR and VR in manufacturing holds tremendous potential for innovation and advancement. Some key trends and developments to watch for include:

- *Enhanced Interactivity*: Future AR and VR technologies are expected to offer enhanced interactivity and realism, enabling more immersive and engaging experiences for users. Advanced haptic feedback, gesture recognition, and eye-tracking technologies (MR) will allow users to interact with virtual objects and environments in more natural and intuitive ways, enhancing training effectiveness and user engagement.

- *Integration with IoT and AI*: AR and VR technologies will increasingly integrate with Internet of Things (IoT) sensors and Artificial Intelligence (AI) algorithms to provide real-time data analytics and insights. IoT-enabled AR glasses, for example, could overlay real-time equipment performance data onto the user's field of view, enabling technicians to monitor machine health and diagnose issues on the shop floor. AI-driven VR simulations could dynamically adapt training scenarios based on user performance and learning objectives, personalizing the training experience for each individual.

- *Industry-specific Applications*: AR and VR technologies will continue to evolve to meet the specific needs and requirements of different manufacturing sectors. From automotive assembly lines to aerospace manufacturing facilities, AR and VR applications will be tailored to address the unique challenges and complexities of each industry, driving productivity, efficiency, and innovation.

- *Accessibility and Affordability*: As AR and VR technologies become more mainstream, they are expected to become increasingly accessible and affordable for manufacturers of all sizes. Advances in hardware, software, and cloud-based services will democratize access to AR and VR tools, allowing small and medium-sized enterprises (SMEs) to leverage these technologies to enhance their operations and competitiveness.

In conclusion, AR and VR technologies are revolutionizing the manufacturing industry by offering innovative solutions to enhance training, maintenance, and design processes. By providing immersive and interactive experiences, AR and VR enable manufacturers to improve productivity, efficiency, and safety while unlocking new opportunities for innovation and growth. As these technologies continue to evolve and mature, they will play an increasingly central role in shaping the future of manufacturing.

SMART MANUFACTURING FOR FACTORIES

Smart Manufacturing and Interconnected Production Systems: Navigate the landscape of smart manufacturing, where interconnected systems drive efficiency. Explore the components of smart factories, implementation challenges, and the keys to success.

- Concept of Smart Manufacturing.
- Components of Smart Factories.
- Implementation Challenges and Success Factors.

INDUSTRY 4.0 REVOLUTION

Smart manufacturing, also known as Industry 4.0, represents a paradigm shift in the way manufacturing processes are conceptualized, executed, and optimized. In this chapter, we will explore the concept of smart manufacturing, delve into the components of smart factories, and discuss the implementation challenges and success factors associated with this transformative approach to manufacturing.

Concept of Smart Manufacturing

Smart manufacturing is a holistic approach to manufacturing that leverages advanced technologies, such as Internet of Things (IoT), Industrial Internet of Things (IIoT), Artificial Intelligence (AI), robotics, and data analytics, to create interconnected and intelligent production systems. At its core, smart manufacturing aims to digitize and optimize every aspect of the manufacturing process, from product design and production to supply chain management and customer service.

The key principles of smart manufacturing include:

- *Connectivity*: Smart manufacturing relies on seamless connectivity between machines, sensors, devices, and systems throughout the production environment. This interconnected network enables real-time data sharing, communication, and collaboration, facilitating agile and responsive manufacturing operations.

- *Data-driven Decision-making*: Smart manufacturing harnesses the power of data analytics and AI to collect, analyze, and interpret vast amounts of data generated by manufacturing processes. By transforming raw data into actionable insights, manufacturers can make informed decisions, optimize performance, and drive continuous improvement.

- *Automation and Robotics*: Automation and robotics play a central role in smart manufacturing, enabling the automation of repetitive tasks, the integration of flexible production lines, and the implementation of autonomous manufacturing systems.

Robots equipped with AI and machine learning capabilities can perform complex tasks with precision and efficiency, enhancing productivity and quality.

- *Predictive Maintenance*: Smart manufacturing utilizes predictive maintenance techniques to monitor equipment health in real-time, predict potential failures, and schedule maintenance proactively. By leveraging IoT sensors and predictive analytics, manufacturers can minimize downtime, reduce maintenance costs, and optimize asset performance.

Components of Smart Factories

Smart factories are the physical embodiment of smart manufacturing principles, where advanced technologies converge to create intelligent and interconnected production systems. The key components of smart factories include:

- *IoT-enabled Sensors and Devices*: Smart factories are equipped with a network of IoT-enabled sensors and devices that collect real-time data on equipment performance, environmental conditions, and production processes. These sensors monitor parameters such as temperature, pressure, vibration, and humidity, providing valuable insights into operational efficiency and performance.

- *Data Analytics and AI*: Smart factories leverage data analytics and AI algorithms to analyze and interpret the vast amounts of data generated by manufacturing processes. Advanced analytics tools can identify patterns, trends, and anomalies in the data, enabling predictive maintenance, process optimization, and quality control.

- *Robotics and Automation*: Smart factories deploy robotics and automation technologies to automate repetitive tasks, streamline production workflows, and improve efficiency. Robots equipped with AI and machine learning capabilities can adapt to changing production requirements, collaborate with human workers, and perform tasks with precision and speed.

- *Digital Twins*: Digital twins are virtual replicas of physical assets, processes, or systems that enable real-time monitoring, simulation, and optimization. Smart factories use digital twins to create virtual models of production lines, equipment, and supply chains, allowing manufacturers to test and optimize processes in a virtual environment before implementation in the real world.

- *Cloud Computing*: Cloud computing enables smart factories to store, process, and analyze large volumes of data in a scalable and cost-effective manner. Cloud-based platforms provide manufacturers with the flexibility to access data and applications from anywhere, facilitating real-time collaboration, remote monitoring, and decision-making.

- *Advanced materials & 3D printing*: The Industrial Revolution has entered a new phase with the advent of advanced materials, which are redefining manufacturing processes and product capabilities. These materials, including high-strength steels, Aluminium alloys, titanium alloys, copper alloys, and composites, offer greater strength, durability, and versatility. Their unique properties allow for the production of parts that are lighter, more robust, and resistant to extreme conditions, which is essential in industries such as aerospace, automotive, medical, defense, and energy. The revolution in the Aluminium and steel industries has been pivotal in shaping modern manufacturing. High-strength steels, with their superior yield and tensile strength, have enabled the production of thinner and lighter components without compromising on durability. This has been particularly transformative in the automotive and construction sectors. Meanwhile, Aluminium alloys, known for their low density and excellent corrosion resistance, have become indispensable in aerospace and automotive applications. The ability to create lightweight yet strong parts has significantly enhanced fuel efficiency and performance in these industries. The integration of 3D printing technology with advanced materials is driving further innovation. 3D printing allows for the precise and efficient creation of complex geometries that would be difficult or impossible to achieve with traditional manufacturing methods. When combined with advanced materials, this technology can produce high-performance parts tailored to specific applications. One of the most promising developments is the use of 3D printing to build inert anodes for the Aluminium industry. Inert anodes, made from advanced materials like ceramics and metal composites, do not consume carbon during the smelting process, thus significantly reducing greenhouse gas emissions and producing oxygen instead of CO_2. Inert anode metallurgical compositions typically consist of materials that resist oxidation and corrosion at the high temperatures encountered during the Aluminium electrolysis process. Common compositions include ceramics like nickel ferrite ($NiFe_2O_4$), copper nickel ferrite ($CuNiFeO_4$), and doped tin oxide (SnO_2), as well as metal-ceramic composites such as Cu-Ni-Fe-O and Ni-Co-Fe-O. Additionally, nickel-based and cobalt-based alloys, known for their high-temperature stability and resistance to oxidation, are used. Conductive ceramics like spinels (e.g., magnesium aluminate) and perovskites (e.g., calcium titanate) also provide a good combination of mechanical strength and electrical conductivity. These advanced materials aim to replace traditional carbon anodes, significantly reducing greenhouse gas emissions and improving the sustainability of Aluminium production. This innovation not only makes the Aluminium production process more environmentally friendly but also enhances the durability and efficiency of the anodes.

Additionally, 3D printing with advanced materials enables the creation of high-strength fibers and ceramics that are essential for reinforcing Aluminium products. These materials provide superior performance characteristics, such as enhanced strength-to-weight ratios, corrosion resistance, and thermal stability, which are crucial for high-demand applications.

The fusion of advanced materials and 3D printing technology marks a significant trend in the ongoing Industrial Revolution. By enabling the production of sophisticated, high-quality components, these advancements are setting new standards in manufacturing efficiency and environmental sustainability, particularly within the Aluminium and steel industries.

Implementation Challenges and Success Factors

Despite the numerous benefits of smart manufacturing, implementing a smart factory can be challenging due to various factors, including:

- *Legacy Systems and Infrastructure*: Many manufacturing facilities have legacy systems and infrastructure that may not be compatible with emerging technologies. Integrating new technologies with existing systems can be complex and require careful planning and investment.

- *Data Security and Privacy*: Smart factories generate and rely on vast amounts of data, raising concerns about data security and privacy. Manufacturers must implement robust cybersecurity measures to protect sensitive data from unauthorized access, hacking, or cyberattacks.

- *Skills and Talent Gap*: Smart manufacturing requires a skilled workforce with expertise in emerging technologies such as data analytics, AI, and robotics. However, there is often a shortage of talent with the necessary skills and experience, requiring manufacturers to invest in training and development programs to upskill their workforce.

- *Interoperability and Standards*: Smart manufacturing involves the integration of diverse technologies and systems from multiple vendors, leading to interoperability challenges. Manufacturers must ensure that different systems can communicate and exchange data seamlessly by adhering to industry standards and protocols.

Despite these challenges, successful implementation of smart manufacturing requires several key success factors, including:

- *Leadership Commitment*: Leadership commitment and support are critical for driving the digital transformation agenda and fostering a culture of innovation and continuous improvement.

- *Strategic Planning*: Manufacturers must develop a clear vision and roadmap for smart manufacturing, aligning technology investments with business objectives and priorities.

- *Collaboration and Partnerships*: Collaboration with technology partners, suppliers, and industry peers can accelerate the implementation of smart manufacturing initiatives by leveraging shared expertise, resources, and best practices.

- *Agile and Iterative Approach*: Smart manufacturing initiatives should be implemented iteratively, allowing for experimentation, learning, and adaptation based on feedback and results.

In conclusion, smart manufacturing represents a transformative approach to manufacturing that leverages advanced technologies to create intelligent and interconnected production systems. By embracing smart manufacturing principles and deploying innovative technologies, manufacturers can enhance operational efficiency, agility, and competitiveness in today's fast-paced and increasingly digital world. Despite the challenges of implementation, the benefits of smart manufacturing far outweigh the risks, offering manufacturers the opportunity to unlock new levels of productivity, innovation, and growth.

EMPOWERING DIGITAL WORKFORCE

Empowering the Digital Workforce: Learn about the critical role of digital skills in manufacturing and the strategies for empowering the workforce. Discover training and development programs that foster engagement and adoption of digital technologies.

- *Importance of Digital Skills in Manufacturing*
- *Training and Development Programs*
- *Strategies for Employee Engagement and Adoption*

Empowering the digital workforce is essential in today's rapidly evolving manufacturing landscape, where advanced technologies and digital tools are reshaping traditional roles and processes. In this chapter, we will explore the importance of digital skills in manufacturing, discuss training and development programs to upskill the workforce, and examine strategies for employee engagement and adoption of digital technologies.

Importance of Digital Skills in Manufacturing

Digital skills have become increasingly important in manufacturing as the industry undergoes digital transformation and adopts Industry 4.0 technologies. In a digitalized manufacturing environment, employees need to possess a range of digital skills to effectively operate, troubleshoot, and optimize advanced technologies such as robotics, automation systems, IoT devices, and data analytics platforms. Some key digital skills required in manufacturing include:

- *Data Literacy*: Employees need to be able to understand and interpret data generated by manufacturing processes, equipment, and systems. This includes basic data analysis skills, such as data visualization, statistical analysis, and trend identification, as well as familiarity with data management tools and software.

- *Technology Proficiency*: Manufacturing employees should be proficient in using digital tools and technologies relevant to their roles, such as computer-aided design (CAD) software, manufacturing execution systems (MES), enterprise resource planning (ERP) software, and collaborative platforms for communication and collaboration.

- *Problem-Solving Skills*: Digital manufacturing environments often present complex technical challenges that require problem-solving skills and critical thinking abilities. Employees need to be able to troubleshoot equipment issues, diagnose problems, and implement solutions in a timely and effective manner.

- *Adaptability and Flexibility*: As manufacturing processes become more automated and interconnected, employees need to be adaptable and flexible in embracing change and learning new technologies. This includes being open to new ways of working, experimenting with emerging technologies, and continuously updating their skills to stay relevant in a rapidly evolving industry.

Training and Development Programs

To equip the workforce with the necessary digital skills, manufacturers should invest in comprehensive training and development programs tailored to the specific needs of their organization and employees. These programs should encompass both technical training on digital tools and technologies and soft skills training to foster a culture of innovation, collaboration, and continuous learning.

Some key components of training and development programs for the digital workforce include:

- *Technical Training*: Technical training programs should cover the use and operation of digital tools and technologies relevant to employees' roles, including hands-on training, demonstrations, and simulations. This may include training on specific software applications, equipment operation, maintenance procedures, and safety protocols.

- *Cross-Functional Training*: Cross-functional training programs can help employees develop a broader understanding of the manufacturing process and their role within the organization. This may include training on related functions such as supply chain management, quality control, and customer service to promote collaboration and cross-functional teamwork.

- *Soft Skills Training*: Soft skills training is essential for fostering a positive work environment and effective communication and collaboration among employees. This may include training on teamwork, problem-solving, communication skills, leadership development, and change management to support the successful implementation of digital initiatives.

- *Continuous Learning*: In addition to formal training programs, manufacturers should encourage a culture of continuous learning and skill development among employees. This may include providing access to online learning resources, webinars, workshops, and conferences, as well as supporting employees in pursuing professional certifications and qualifications relevant to their roles.

Strategies for Employee Engagement and Adoption

In addition to providing training and development opportunities, manufacturers should implement strategies to engage employees and promote the adoption of digital technologies. Employee engagement is crucial for ensuring that digital initiatives are embraced and integrated into daily workflows effectively.

Some strategies for promoting employee engagement and adoption of digital technologies include:

- *Leadership Support*: Leadership support and visible commitment to digital transformation initiatives are essential for gaining buy-in from employees and fostering a culture of innovation and continuous improvement. Leaders should communicate the vision, goals, and benefits of digital transformation initiatives and actively involve employees in the planning and implementation process.

- *Clear Communication*: Clear and transparent communication is key to ensuring that employees understand the purpose, objectives, and expected outcomes of digital initiatives. Manufacturers should provide regular updates, feedback, and opportunities for dialogue to address any concerns or questions employees may have.

- *Employee Involvement*: Involving employees in the decision-making process and soliciting their input and feedback can increase ownership and commitment to digital transformation initiatives. Manufacturers should create opportunities for employees to participate in pilot projects, process improvements, and cross-functional teams to drive innovation and collaboration.

- *Recognition and Rewards*: Recognizing and rewarding employees for their contributions to digital transformation initiatives can help reinforce desired behaviors and motivate continued engagement. Manufacturers should acknowledge and celebrate successes, milestones, and achievements related to digital adoption and performance improvements.

- *Training and Support*: Providing ongoing training, support, and resources to employees is essential for building confidence and competence in using digital tools and technologies. Manufacturers should offer on-the-job training, coaching, mentoring, and technical assistance to help employees overcome challenges and barriers to adoption.

In conclusion, empowering the digital workforce is essential for manufacturers to thrive in today's digitalized manufacturing environment. By investing in training and development programs, fostering employee engagement, and promoting the adoption of digital technologies, manufacturers can equip their workforce with the skills, knowledge, and mindset needed to succeed in the era of Industry 4.0.

By empowering employees to embrace digital transformation, manufacturers can drive innovation, improve productivity, and remain competitive in an increasingly digital world.

TRANSFORMATION CHALLENGES AND SOLUTIONS

Overcoming Challenges in Digital Transformation: Identify common challenges in digital transformation and explore strategies for overcoming resistance. Draw inspiration from successful case studies and learn best practices for navigating the transformation journey.

- *Common Challenges in Digital Transformation.*
- *Strategies for Mitigation and Overcoming Resistance.*
- *Case Studies of Successful Transformation Initiatives.*

Digital transformation has become imperative for manufacturing organizations seeking to remain competitive in today's rapidly evolving business landscape. However, the journey towards digitalization is not without its challenges. In this chapter, we will explore some common challenges in digital transformation, strategies for mitigating these challenges, and examine a case study of a successful transformation initiative.

Common Challenges in Digital Transformation

- *Legacy Systems and Infrastructure*: One of the most significant challenges in digital transformation is the presence of legacy systems and infrastructure that may not be compatible with modern digital technologies. Upgrading or replacing legacy systems can be complex, time-consuming, and costly, posing a significant barrier to digital transformation initiatives.

- *Resistance to Change*: Resistance to change is a common challenge encountered in digital transformation efforts. Employees may be hesitant to embrace new technologies or processes due to fear of job displacement, lack of understanding, or concerns about increased workload. Overcoming resistance and fostering a culture of innovation and collaboration are essential for successful digital transformation.

- *Data Security and Privacy Concerns*: As organizations digitize their operations and collect vast amounts of data, data security and privacy concerns become paramount. Ensuring the confidentiality, integrity, and availability of data while complying with regulatory requirements can be challenging, particularly in industries with stringent data protection regulations.

- *Skills Gap and Talent Shortages*: Digital transformation requires a workforce with the skills and expertise to leverage new technologies effectively. However, many organizations face challenges in recruiting, retaining, and upskilling employees with the necessary digital skills, leading to a talent shortage and skills gap that hinders transformation efforts.

- *Integration and Interoperability*: Integrating diverse digital technologies and systems to create a seamless digital ecosystem can be challenging, particularly when dealing with proprietary or incompatible solutions. Achieving interoperability between different systems and platforms is essential for realizing the full potential of digital transformation initiatives.

Strategies for Mitigation and Overcoming Resistance

- *Leadership Commitment and Vision*: Strong leadership commitment and vision are critical for driving digital transformation initiatives forward. Leaders should articulate a clear vision for digital transformation, communicate its importance, and lead by example to inspire and motivate employees to embrace change.

- *Stakeholder Engagement and Communication*: Engaging stakeholders at all levels of the organization and communicating effectively about the benefits and objectives of digital transformation initiatives are essential for gaining buy-in and support. Organizations should create opportunities for dialogue, address concerns, and involve employees in the decision-making process.

- *Change Management and Training*: Implementing robust change management processes and providing comprehensive training and support to employees are essential for overcoming resistance to change. Organizations should invest in change management resources, such as change agents, training programs, and communication campaigns, to facilitate smooth transitions and minimize disruptions.

- *Agile and Iterative Approach*: Adopting an agile and iterative approach to digital transformation allows organizations to experiment, learn, and adapt quickly to changing requirements and circumstances. By breaking down transformation initiatives into smaller, manageable projects and iterating based on feedback and results, organizations can reduce risk and increase the likelihood of success.

- *Collaboration and Partnerships*: Collaborating with external partners, such as technology vendors, consultants, and industry experts, can provide organizations with access to specialized expertise, resources, and best practices. By forming strategic partnerships and leveraging external networks, organizations can accelerate their digital transformation journey and overcome internal barriers.

Case Study: Successful Transformation Initiative at AHMSA Manufacturing Company

AHMSA Steel Manufacturing Company, a leading steel manufacturer, embarked on a digital transformation journey to modernize its manufacturing operations and improve efficiency, quality, and agility. Despite facing several challenges along the way, AHMSA successfully implemented a series of transformation initiatives that revolutionized its production processes and established it as a leader in digital manufacturing.

One of the key challenges AHMSA encountered was resistance to change from employees accustomed to traditional manufacturing methods. To overcome this challenge, AHMSA invested heavily in change management initiatives, including comprehensive training programs, employee engagement activities, and communication campaigns. By involving employees in the planning and implementation process and providing them with the necessary skills and support, AHMSA was able to foster a culture of innovation and collaboration that facilitated the adoption of digital technologies.

Another challenge AHMSA faced was legacy systems and infrastructure that were incompatible with modern digital technologies. To address this challenge, AHMSA undertook a phased approach to digital transformation, prioritizing areas where technology could have the most significant impact and gradually modernizing its systems and processes over time. By taking a pragmatic and iterative approach, AHMSA minimized disruptions and managed risks while laying the foundation for future growth and innovation.

One of the key success factors of AHMSA's transformation initiative was strong leadership commitment and vision. The executive team at AHMSA championed digital transformation as a strategic priority, providing the necessary resources, support, and direction to drive the initiative forward. By articulating a clear vision for the future and leading by example, AHMSA's leadership instilled confidence and enthusiasm among employees and stakeholders, fostering a sense of purpose and direction that propelled the transformation efforts forward. Through a combination of leadership commitment, stakeholder engagement, change management, and strategic partnerships, AHMSA steel Manufacturing Company was able to overcome the challenges of digital transformation and achieve its objectives. Today, AHMSA stands as a testament to the transformative power of digital technologies in manufacturing, demonstrating the immense value that can be unlocked through innovation, collaboration, and perseverance in the face of adversity.

FUTURE TRENDS AND SUSTAINABLE GROWTH

Future Trends and Innovations in Manufacturing: Peer into the future of manufacturing and anticipate emerging trends and innovations. Explore the potential impact of new technologies on the industry and prepare for the next wave of innovation.

- *Emerging Technologies and Innovations.*
- *Potential Impact on Manufacturing Industry.*
- *Anticipated Trends in the Coming Years.*

In the rapidly evolving landscape of manufacturing, staying abreast of future trends and innovations is essential for organizations to remain competitive and thrive in the digital age. As technology continues to advance at an unprecedented pace, manufacturing industries are witnessing the emergence of groundbreaking innovations that promise to revolutionize processes, enhance efficiency, and drive sustainable growth. In this chapter, we delve into the future trends and innovations shaping the manufacturing industry, exploring emerging technologies, their potential impact, and anticipated trends in the coming years.

Emerging Technologies and Innovations

The manufacturing industry is at the forefront of technological innovation, with several emerging technologies poised to transform traditional processes and operations. One such innovation is additive manufacturing, also known as 3D printing, which enables the production of complex geometries and customized parts with unprecedented speed and precision. Additive manufacturing has the potential to disrupt traditional manufacturing methods by reducing lead times, minimizing material waste, and enabling on-demand production.

Another transformative technology gaining traction in the manufacturing sector is artificial intelligence (AI) and machine learning. AI-powered systems can analyze vast amounts of data, identify patterns, and make autonomous decisions, enhancing efficiency, and enabling predictive maintenance, quality control, and demand forecasting. Machine learning algorithms can optimize production processes, improve product quality, and drive continuous improvement initiatives.

Furthermore, the Internet of Things (IoT) is revolutionizing manufacturing by connecting physical devices, machines, and sensors to the internet, enabling real-time monitoring, control, and optimization of production environments. IoT-enabled smart factories can collect and analyze data from various sources, providing insights into equipment performance, energy consumption, and production efficiency. By leveraging IoT technologies, manufacturers can achieve higher levels of automation, productivity, and agility.

Additionally, advanced robotics and automation technologies are reshaping the manufacturing landscape by automating repetitive tasks, increasing throughput, and enhancing workplace safety. Collaborative robots, or cobots, are designed to work alongside human operators, performing tasks that require precision, dexterity, and flexibility. Robotic process automation (RPA) is streamlining administrative processes, reducing errors, and improving operational efficiency across various functions, from supply chain management to finance and accounting.

Potential Impact on the Manufacturing Industry

The adoption of emerging technologies and innovations is expected to have a profound impact on the manufacturing industry, revolutionizing processes, business models, and value chains. One of the primary benefits of these technologies is increased efficiency and productivity, as automation, AI, and IoT/IIoT enable faster production cycles, reduced downtime, and optimized resource utilization. Manufacturers can achieve higher output volumes, faster time-to-market, and improved cost-effectiveness, driving competitive advantage and market differentiation.

Moreover, emerging technologies enable greater customization and personalization of products, catering to evolving consumer preferences and market demands. Additive manufacturing allows for the production of complex, customized components with minimal tooling and setup costs, enabling manufacturers to offer tailor-made solutions to customers. AI-powered analytics can analyze consumer data, predict trends, and personalize products and services to meet individual needs, driving customer satisfaction and loyalty.

Furthermore, the adoption of emerging technologies is reshaping supply chains, enabling greater visibility, transparency, and resilience. IoT sensors and blockchain technology can track and trace products throughout the supply chain, providing real-time insights into inventory levels, shipping status, and product authenticity. Smart contracts powered by blockchain can automate transactions, streamline procurement processes, and mitigate risks associated with counterfeit products and supply chain disruptions.

Anticipated Trends in the Coming Years

Looking ahead, several key trends are expected to shape the future of manufacturing, driven by advancements in technology, changing consumer preferences, and evolving regulatory landscapes. One such trend is the rise of **sustainable manufacturing practices**, as companies increasingly prioritize environmental stewardship and resource efficiency. Manufacturers are embracing circular economy principles, reducing waste, and adopting renewable energy sources to minimize their environmental footprint. Current trendy such are Celestial energy utilized products and Green products from recyclable.

Additionally, the integration of **digital twins** into manufacturing processes is anticipated to gain momentum, enabling virtual simulations, predictive modeling, and optimization of production systems. Digital twins create virtual replicas of physical assets, allowing manufacturers to visualize, analyze, and optimize processes in real-time, improving operational efficiency and reducing time-to-market.

Moreover, the convergence of physical and digital worlds, often referred to as cyber-physical systems, will continue to accelerate, blurring the boundaries between traditional manufacturing and digital technologies. Cyber-physical systems enable seamless communication and collaboration between machines, humans, and data, enabling adaptive, responsive, and interconnected production environments.

Furthermore, the democratization of technology is expected to empower smaller manufacturers and startups, enabling them to compete with larger incumbents by leveraging cloud computing, open-source software, and digital platforms. As technology becomes more accessible and affordable, innovation ecosystems will flourish, driving entrepreneurship, collaboration, and knowledge sharing across industries.

In conclusion, the future of manufacturing holds immense promise, driven by emerging technologies, innovative business models, and shifting consumer expectations. By embracing these trends and innovations, manufacturers can unlock new opportunities for growth, sustainability, and resilience in an increasingly competitive global market. As we embark on this journey of digital transformation, let us embrace change, foster collaboration, and harness the power of innovation to shape a brighter future for the manufacturing industry.

CASE STUDIES OF TRANSFORMATION

Case Studies: Real-World Examples of Successful Digital Transformation in Manufacturing: Dive into real-world case studies from various industries, showcasing successful digital transformation initiatives. Extract valuable insights, implementation strategies, and best practices for your own transformation journey.

- *Case Studies from Various Industries.*
- *Implementation Strategies and Lessons Learned.*
- *Best Practices for Successful Transformation.*

INDUSTRY 4.0 REVOLUTION

Digital transformation has become a critical imperative for manufacturers seeking to remain competitive in today's rapidly evolving business landscape. Across various industries, organizations are leveraging digital technologies to optimize processes, enhance efficiency, and drive innovation. In this chapter, we examine real-world case studies of successful digital transformation initiatives in manufacturing, exploring implementation strategies, lessons learned, and best practices for achieving sustainable transformation.

Case Studies from Various Industries

- *Ahmsa Steel Company*: Ahmsa Steel Company, a leading steel manufacturer, embarked on a digital transformation journey to enhance operational efficiency and competitiveness. By implementing IIoT sensors and predictive analytics, Ahmsa Steel Company optimized equipment performance, reduced downtime, and improved maintenance processes. Real-time monitoring and predictive maintenance enabled proactive interventions, ensuring uninterrupted production and cost savings.

- *TechSoft Automotive*: TechSoft Automotive, a global automotive supplier, embraced automation and robotics to streamline manufacturing processes and improve product quality. By deploying collaborative robots (cobots) on assembly lines, TechSoft Automotive increased production throughput, minimized errors, and enhanced workplace safety. Automation of repetitive tasks enabled employees to focus on higher-value activities, driving productivity and innovation. Example: Oneway Robotics – As a lead volunteer at Expo 2020, I witnessed their cobot's remarkable and flawless patrol and delivery functions.

- *PharmaTech Pharmaceuticals*: PharmaTech Pharmaceuticals, a pharmaceutical manufacturing company, adopted blockchain technology to enhance supply chain transparency and traceability. By leveraging blockchain-enabled platforms, PharmaTech Pharmaceuticals ensured the authenticity and integrity of pharmaceutical products, reducing the risk of counterfeiting and ensuring compliance with regulatory requirements. Blockchain technology facilitated end-to-end visibility into the supply chain, enabling rapid response to quality issues and recalls. Example: MediLedger Network.

- *AeroTech Aerospace*: AeroTech Aerospace, a leading aerospace manufacturer, implemented digital twin technology to optimize aircraft design and manufacturing processes. By creating virtual replicas of aircraft components and systems, AeroTech Aerospace simulated and validated designs, reducing time-to-market and minimizing development costs. Digital twins enabled collaborative design reviews and iterative improvements, ensuring product quality and performance. Example – Sedaro – The Sedaro digital twins can deliver massive value across teams and across the system lifecycle.

Implementation Strategies and Lessons Learned

- *Clear Vision and Leadership*: Successful digital transformation initiatives require strong leadership and a clear vision for change. Organizations must articulate their digital strategy, set clear objectives, and secure executive sponsorship to drive alignment and commitment across the organization.

- *Agile and Iterative Approach*: Adopting an agile and iterative approach to digital transformation allows organizations to quickly adapt to changing market dynamics and technology advancements. By breaking down transformation initiatives into manageable projects and conducting frequent reviews and adjustments, organizations can minimize risks and accelerate time-to-value.

- *Talent Development and Change Management*: Building digital capabilities and fostering a culture of innovation are essential for successful transformation. Organizations must invest in talent development programs, provide training and resources to employees, and actively engage stakeholders throughout the change process. Effective change management practices, such as communication, collaboration, and empowerment, can mitigate resistance and promote adoption of digital technologies

- *Ecosystem Collaboration*: Collaboration with ecosystem partners, including technology vendors, startups, research institutions, and industry associations, can accelerate innovation and drive shared value creation. By leveraging external expertise, resources, and networks, organizations can access best practices, co-develop solutions, and stay ahead of industry trends.

- *Continuous Improvement and Measurement*: Continuous improvement is essential for sustaining digital transformation success. Organizations must establish metrics and KPIs to monitor progress, measure outcomes, and identify areas for optimization. Regular performance reviews, post-implementation evaluations, and feedback mechanisms enable organizations to iterate and evolve their digital strategies over time.

Best Practices for Successful Transformation

- *Customer-Centric Approach*: Align digital transformation initiatives with customer needs and preferences to drive customer satisfaction and loyalty. By understanding customer pain points, preferences, and behaviors, organizations can prioritize investments and innovations that deliver tangible value and differentiate their offerings in the market.

- *Data-Driven Decision-Making*: Harness the power of data analytics and business intelligence to inform decision-making and drive operational excellence. By leveraging real-time data insights, organizations can identify trends, anticipate demand, and optimize resource allocation, enabling proactive decision-making and agile responsiveness to market dynamics.

- *Scalable and Modular Architecture*: Design digital solutions with scalability and flexibility in mind to accommodate future growth and evolving business requirements. Adopting modular architectures, open standards, and interoperable systems allows organizations to integrate new technologies, applications, and capabilities seamlessly, enabling agility and adaptability in a rapidly changing environment.

- *Risk Management and Cybersecurity*: Prioritize cybersecurity and risk management to protect digital assets, data, and intellectual property from cyber threats and breaches. Implement robust security protocols, encryption technologies, and access controls to safeguard sensitive information and ensure compliance with regulatory requirements. Proactive risk assessment, monitoring, and incident response capabilities are essential for mitigating risks and minimizing disruptions to operations.

- *Continuous Innovation and Collaboration*: Foster a culture of innovation and collaboration to drive continuous improvement and competitive advantage. Encourage experimentation, knowledge sharing, and cross-functional collaboration to identify new opportunities, challenge conventional thinking, and drive breakthrough innovations. By empowering employees to contribute ideas, experiment with new technologies, and embrace change, organizations can unlock creativity, resilience, and agility in the face of uncertainty.

Conclusion

Digital transformation is reshaping the manufacturing industry, unlocking new opportunities for innovation, growth, and competitiveness. By embracing digital technologies and adopting a strategic approach to transformation, organizations can optimize processes, enhance agility, and create value for customers and stakeholders. Real-world case studies highlight the diverse applications and benefits of digital transformation across industries, serving as valuable learning experiences for organizations embarking on their own transformation journeys. By implementing best practices, leveraging lessons learned, and fostering a culture of innovation and collaboration, organizations can navigate the complexities of digital transformation successfully and position themselves for long-term success in the digital age.

STARTUP'S ROLE IN MANUFACTURING

Future Trends, Opportunities in Manufacturing, and Startup Ecosystem: Discover future trends and opportunities in manufacturing, with a focus on the role of the startup ecosystem. Explore collaborative opportunities between startups and established manufacturers, driving innovation and growth.

- *Overview of Future Trends and Opportunities.*
- *Role of Startup Ecosystem in Driving Innovation.*
- *Collaborative Opportunities for Startups and Established Manufacturers.*

In the rapidly evolving landscape of manufacturing, staying ahead of future trends and embracing emerging opportunities is essential for sustainable growth and competitiveness. Drawing insights from the books "MYOPIC STARTUP" and "BUSINESS SUCCESS CHECKLIST" authored by Aeknath Mishra, author explore the future trajectory of the manufacturing industry and the pivotal role played by the startup ecosystem in driving innovation and collaboration.

1. Overview of Future Trends and Opportunities

The manufacturing industry is undergoing a profound transformation fueled by advancements in technology, changing consumer preferences, and evolving market dynamics. Future trends indicate a shift towards smart manufacturing, digitalization, and sustainable practices. Companies are increasingly leveraging technologies such as artificial intelligence, robotics, and IoT to optimize operations, improve efficiency, and deliver customized products and services. Furthermore, the rise of additive manufacturing, also known as 3D printing, is revolutionizing traditional production methods by enabling rapid prototyping, customization, and decentralized manufacturing.

As highlighted in "MYOPIC STARTUP" and "BUSINESS SUCCESS CHECKLIST," embracing these future trends requires a proactive approach to innovation and adaptation. Companies must invest in research and development, cultivate a culture of continuous learning, and foster collaboration with industry partners and startups to capitalize on emerging opportunities.

Norway's aluminium and renewable energy firm Hydro recently received an award at the 2023 UN Climate Change Conference in the United Arab Emirates for its pioneering work on green aluminium. The proprietary technology could fully decarbonize aluminium smelting. The company is working on offering a different type of technology to replace the Hall-Héroult process, its mostly with advance material to produce inert anode. Instead of emitting CO_2 during the electrolysis stage, Hydro's HalZero technology keeps the carbon and chlorine in a closed loop, eliminating CO_2 emissions and emitting only oxygen.

Hydro's HalZero technology is an innovative solution developed by the Norwegian Aluminium company Hydro to address environmental concerns and improve sustainability in the Aluminium smelting process. HalZero stands for "halve emissions to zero," emphasizing Hydro's ambitious goal to drastically reduce greenhouse gas emissions associated with Aluminium production.

The HalZero technology focuses on implementing inert anodes in Aluminium electrolysis cells, replacing traditional carbon-based anodes. In conventional Aluminium smelting, carbon anodes are consumed during the process, releasing carbon dioxide (CO_2) emissions. In contrast, inert anodes do not consume carbon and instead produce oxygen (O_2) when exposed to the high temperatures of the electrolysis cell.

By adopting HalZero technology and transitioning to inert anodes, Hydro aims to significantly reduce CO_2 emissions from its Aluminium production operations. This shift towards inert anodes is a crucial step in making Aluminium production more sustainable and environmentally friendly. Additionally, Hydro's HalZero technology aligns with global efforts to combat climate change and reduce the carbon footprint of industrial processes.

2. Purer Recycled Aluminium Revolutionizes Sustainability in Metal Industry

Recycling aluminium offers a significant environmental advantage, consuming 95% less energy compared to primary production methods while often being more cost-effective. However, the quality of recycled aluminium has historically been hindered by impurities and alloying elements, restricting its usage in high-precision applications like electronic components and electric vehicles. Addressing this challenge, researchers in the US are spearheading an innovative solution to extract metal impurities from recycled aluminium, paving the way for its expanded use across various industries. This development not only enhances the quality of recycled aluminium but also aligns with global sustainability goals, offering a promising pathway towards reducing carbon emissions and promoting a circular economy.

This groundbreaking initiative, supported by a 170-member public-private partnership and partially funded by the United States Department of Energy, underscores the collaborative effort to advance sustainable technologies in the metal industry. While specific details of the solution remain confidential, its potential to elevate the sustainability and versatility of recycled aluminium signifies a significant stride towards a greener and more efficient aluminium production process. By unlocking the full potential of recycled aluminium, this innovation contributes to the broader objective of achieving environmental stewardship and resource efficiency in the manufacturing sector.

3. Role of Startup Ecosystem in Driving Innovation

The startup ecosystem plays a pivotal role in driving innovation and disruption in the manufacturing industry. Startups are nimble, agile, and unencumbered by legacy systems, allowing them to experiment with novel ideas and technologies. In the Primary Steel and Primary Aluminium sectors, collaborations with startup founders have led to remarkable digital innovations, illustrating the transformative impact of such partnerships. Few Real-Life Examples are:

Predictive Maintenance Solutions: Startups specializing in predictive maintenance technology have partnered with Primary Steel companies to develop advanced algorithms that predict equipment failures before they occur. By leveraging machine learning and IoT sensors, these solutions optimize maintenance schedules, reduce downtime, and enhance overall operational efficiency.

Recycling Optimization Platforms: In the Primary Aluminium industry, startups have collaborated with industry leaders to create recycling optimization platforms. These platforms utilize data analytics and machine learning algorithms to optimize the recycling process, increasing material recovery rates and reducing waste. Such innovations contribute to sustainability efforts and resource conservation.

Supply Chain Transparency Solutions: Startups focused on supply chain transparency have partnered with Primary Steel and Primary Aluminium companies to develop blockchain-based solutions. These solutions enhance traceability throughout the supply chain, ensuring ethical sourcing practices and promoting transparency for stakeholders. By enabling real-time tracking of materials, these innovations improve accountability and trust within the industry.

Energy Efficiency Technologies: Startups specializing in energy efficiency technologies have collaborated with Primary Steel and Primary Aluminium manufacturers to implement innovative solutions for reducing energy consumption. Through the adoption of smart sensors, automation, and optimization algorithms, these technologies optimize energy usage, leading to cost savings and environmental benefits. In a groundbreaking partnership, Rio Tinto is teaming up with the Australian Renewable Energy Agency (ARENA) to revolutionize sustainability practices by investigating the viability of hydrogen as a substitute for fossil fuels in alumina refineries. This forward-thinking initiative targets emissions reduction in the energy-intensive refining phase of the aluminium supply chain. ARENA emphasizes the transformative potential of clean hydrogen in mitigating emissions, paving the way for the production of eco-friendly aluminium. This collaboration underscores the imperative of adopting innovative clean energy solutions to meet environmental goals within the mining and manufacturing industries.

In "JUAN", author explores the journey of a startup and his transformative impact on various industries, including manufacturing. Startups bring fresh perspectives, innovative solutions, and a hunger for growth, making them invaluable partners for established manufacturers seeking to stay ahead of the curve. Through collaboration and co-creation, startups and established manufacturers can leverage each other's strengths to drive mutual success.

4. Collaborative Opportunities for Startups and Manufacturers

Collaboration between startups and established manufacturers presents a wealth of opportunities for innovation, growth, and market expansion. Established manufacturers bring industry expertise, resources, and infrastructure, while startups contribute disruptive technologies, agility, and entrepreneurial spirit. Together, they can co-create solutions that address complex challenges, unlock new revenue streams, and deliver value to customers.

Here are few examples of collaborations between startups and established manufacturers:

BMW and Carbon: BMW collaborated with the 3D printing startup Carbon to incorporate additive manufacturing technology into their production processes. Together, they developed the Digital Light Synthesis (DLS) technology, which allows for the production of high-performance automotive components with complex geometries and improved durability.

GE and Local Motors: General Electric (GE) partnered with the startup Local Motors to create the world's first 3D-printed jet engine. The collaboration led to the development of the GE9X engine for Boeing's 777X aircraft, which features 3D-printed components that are lighter, more fuel-efficient, and faster to produce than traditional manufacturing methods.

Siemens and LO3 Energy: Siemens collaborated with the startup LO3 Energy to develop a blockchain-based peer-to-peer energy trading platform. The platform allows consumers to buy and sell excess renewable energy directly with their neighbors, bypassing traditional energy suppliers and promoting decentralized energy generation and distribution.

Nike and Flex: Nike partnered with the manufacturing services company Flex to develop advanced footwear manufacturing technologies. Together, they created the Flex Speedfactory, a state-of-the-art facility equipped with robotic automation and 3D printing capabilities to produce customized athletic shoes with shorter lead times and reduced environmental impact.

Toyota and Preferred Networks: Toyota collaborated with the Japanese startup Preferred Networks to develop autonomous vehicle technology. Together, they created the Toyota Research Institute Advanced Development (TRI-AD) division, which focuses on developing artificial intelligence and robotics solutions for autonomous driving systems.

Toyota and Tesla: Toyota collaborated with Tesla to incorporate Tesla's electric powertrain technology into Toyota's vehicles, leading to the development of electric and hybrid models such as the Toyota RAV4 EV and the Toyota Prius Plug-in Hybrid.

IBM and Maersk: IBM collaborated with Maersk, a global shipping company, to develop TradeLens, a blockchain-based platform for global trade. TradeLens digitizes and streamlines the supply chain, allowing for greater transparency, security, and efficiency in global trade operations.

Airbus and Local Motors: Airbus partnered with Local Motors to launch the Airbus Cargo Drone Challenge, inviting designers and engineers to submit concepts for autonomous cargo drones. The collaboration resulted in innovative drone designs that could potentially revolutionize the logistics industry.

Siemens and Carbon Clean Solutions: Siemens collaborated with Carbon Clean Solutions to develop carbon capture technology for industrial applications. The partnership aims to reduce carbon emissions from industries such as cement, steel, and power generation, contributing to global efforts to combat climate change.

Alcoa and CarbonCure Technologies: Alcoa, a leading aluminium producer, partnered with CarbonCure Technologies, a startup specializing in carbon capture and utilization, to develop carbon dioxide (CO_2) sequestration technology for concrete production. This collaboration aims to reduce CO_2 emissions in the construction industry by injecting recycled CO_2 into concrete, enhancing its strength and sustainability.

ArcelorMittal and Xometry: ArcelorMittal, one of the world's largest steel producers, collaborated with Xometry, a startup offering on-demand manufacturing services, to streamline the procurement process for custom steel parts. Through Xometry's platform, customers can access ArcelorMittal's extensive range of steel materials and specifications, enabling rapid prototyping and production of steel components for various industries.

Novelis and Ampcera: Novelis, a global leader in aluminium rolling and recycling, partnered with Ampcera, a startup specializing in solid-state electrolyte technology, to develop next-generation batteries for electric vehicles (EVs). By leveraging Ampcera's solid-state electrolyte materials, Novelis aims to enhance the performance and safety of EV batteries, supporting the transition to sustainable mobility solutions.

Norsk Hydro and Heliogen: Norsk Hydro, a major aluminium producer, collaborated with Heliogen, a startup focused on concentrated solar power technology, to explore the use of solar energy in aluminium smelting operations. This partnership aims to reduce greenhouse gas emissions and energy costs in aluminium production by harnessing Heliogen's advanced solar thermal technology to generate heat for smelting processes.

Tata Steel and Velo3D: Tata Steel, Where I served for a long duration, a leading steel manufacturer, partnered with Velo3D, a startup specializing in metal additive manufacturing, to enhance the production of complex steel components for aerospace and automotive applications. By leveraging Velo3D's advanced metal 3D printing technology, Tata Steel aims to reduce lead times, minimize material waste, and optimize the performance of steel parts for critical applications.

Mood based facial attendance camera with gate management and scanning: Incorporating Industry 4.0 technologies, our smart factory plan introduces a mood-based facial attendance camera integrated with gate management and scanning. This innovative system uses advanced facial recognition and emotion detection algorithms to record employee attendance and monitor their well-being. Coupled with gate management, it ensures secure and efficient access control, reducing bottlenecks and enhancing workplace safety. The scanning feature adds another layer of security by verifying employee credentials and tracking entry and exit times. This seamless integration of AI and IoT technologies fosters a more responsive, secure, and efficient working environment, aligning with modern smart factory standards.

Smart tower to capture change in Noise, Temperature and images for predictive maintenance: Introducing SmartFactory Solutions' innovative Industry 4.0-enabled smart tower for predictive maintenance. Our tower captures real-time changes in noise levels, temperature fluctuations, and images of machinery, providing invaluable insights for proactive maintenance. Leveraging IoT and AI, this tower monitors equipment health, detects anomalies, and predicts potential failures before they occur, minimizing downtime and optimizing productivity. With seamless integration into existing factory systems, SmartFactory Solutions' predictive maintenance tower empowers manufacturers to enhance equipment reliability, extend asset lifespan, and streamline maintenance operations, ensuring maximum efficiency and profitability in the era of smart manufacturing.

Smart real time maintenance schedule ERP: Enter the era of seamless maintenance with SmartFactory Solutions' Industry 4.0-enabled real-time maintenance schedule ERP. Our advanced system integrates IoT sensors, AI algorithms, and cloud-based ERP software to create a dynamic maintenance schedule tailored to your factory's needs. By continuously monitoring equipment health, predicting maintenance requirements, and optimizing scheduling in real-time, our ERP ensures minimal downtime, maximum efficiency, and cost savings. With intuitive dashboards and predictive analytics, manufacturers gain unprecedented insights into their operations, empowering them to make data-driven decisions and stay ahead in the rapidly evolving landscape of smart manufacturing.

Flue Gas Stack monitoring tower: Stack monitoring for emission and production control. EmissionTech Solutions revolutionizes the aluminium industry's emission by flue gas stacks monitoring with IoT, AI, and blockchain. Our system provides real-time tracking, analysis, and optimization, aiding decarbonization and compliance. Advanced imaging sensors monitor CO_2, NO_x, and particulate matter, while AI offers insights and predictive maintenance. Blockchain ensures transparency and collaboration, aligning with global standards. With 3% of CO_2 emissions attributed to aluminium, our solution addresses urgent decarbonization needs, enhancing sustainability and competitiveness. Revenue from subscriptions, data services, and certification supports our mission. EmissionTech aims to expand to other heavy industries, driving industrial decarbonization for a sustainable future.

Intelligent Vehicle-Mounted Monitoring Devices: SmartFactory Solutions offers advanced Industry 4.0-enabled vehicle-mounted devices for heavy manufacturing industries like aluminium and steel. These intelligent devices capture and analyze data on faults and flaws in real-time, providing predictive maintenance insights. By integrating IoT sensors and AI algorithms, our system ensures accurate fault detection and immediate maintenance scheduling, significantly reducing downtime and operational disruptions. The seamless real-time data transmission to our cloud-based ERP system allows for proactive management and optimization of maintenance tasks, enhancing overall efficiency and productivity. Upgrade to SmartFactory Solutions and drive your manufacturing operations into the future of smart maintenance.

In "MYOPIC STARTUP" and "BUSINESS SUCCESS CHECKLIST," Aeknath Mishra emphasizes the importance of strategic partnerships and alliances in navigating the competitive landscape. By forging collaborative relationships with startups, established manufacturers can access cutting-edge technologies, explore new markets, and accelerate their innovation journey. Joint ventures, incubator programs, and technology scouting initiatives are some of the avenues through which collaboration can thrive, thus boost digital transformation initiatives.

List of Startups with Cutting-Edge Technologies:

These startups not only enhance operational efficiencies but also pioneer solutions leading to significant cost reductions, improved productivity, and enhanced decision-making capabilities.

- Leucine AI - Streamlines development workflows by replacing paper-based records with AI-powered digital twins.

- DroneDeploy - Platform used in manufacturing industries and renewable energy for reality capture using drones, robots, and 360 cameras. The data is then analyzed with AI to enhance efficiency and decision-making.

- Blackshark.ai - Utilizes machine learning to extract infrastructure insights from global satellite and aerial imagery.

- KorrAI - Combines AI, ML, drone surveys, and satellite data to track and manage resources in mining and industries, enabling remote monitoring.

- RobCo - Offers affordable robotics automation for metal manufacturing industries. Their platform simplifies operations with remote robot management and a low-code approach, eliminating complex programming needs.

- Mujin - Utilizes a range of perception, planning, and control algorithms in their Controller to digitize the physical world. This technology enables autonomous operation of robots and industrial machinery, automating tasks in challenging environments at metal manufacturing industries.

- ANNEA - Climate tech startup utilizing AI to generate 3D models or basic data visualizations for monitoring purposes.

In conclusion, the future of manufacturing lies in embracing technological innovation, fostering collaboration, and cultivating a culture of agility and adaptability. By staying abreast of future trends, leveraging the startup ecosystem, and embracing collaborative opportunities, manufacturers can position themselves for long-term success in an increasingly digital and competitive environment. As highlighted in the insightful books by Aeknath Mishra, the journey towards future readiness requires vision, courage, and a commitment to continuous learning and innovation.

BOOK PITCH

Industry 4.0 Revolution: How Startups Empower Digital Transformation in Industries through Digital Transformation is a groundbreaking book that provides invaluable insights into the transformative power of Industry 4.0 in the manufacturing sector. With its comprehensive coverage of key concepts, emerging technologies, and real-world case studies, this book is essential reading for industry professionals, policymakers, academics, startup founder's and anyone interested in the future of manufacturing.

In today's rapidly evolving business landscape, staying ahead of the curve is more important than ever. "Industry 4.0 Revolution" offer readers a roadmap to navigate the complexities of Industry 4.0 and harness its full potential for organizational growth and competitiveness. From understanding the fundamentals of digital transformation to exploring cutting-edge technologies such as IoT, robotics, and predictive analytics, this book equips readers with the knowledge and tools they need to thrive in the digital age.

One of the book's key strengths lies in its practical approach to addressing real-world challenges and opportunities. Through insightful case studies and examples from leading manufacturing companies, readers gain valuable insights into how Industry 4.0 is reshaping traditional business models, driving operational excellence, and unlocking new sources of value. Whether you're a seasoned industry veteran or a newcomer to the field, "Industry 4.0 Revolution" offers something for everyone.

The book's marketing and sales pitch focuses on three key points

- *Comprehensive Coverage*: "Industry 4.0 Revolution" covers a wide range of topics related to Industry 4.0, making it a comprehensive resource for anyone looking to deepen their understanding of the digital transformation of manufacturing. From automation and robotics to data analytics and supply chain optimization, each chapter provides actionable insights and best practices that readers can apply to their own organizations.

- *Practical Insights*: Unlike other books that focus solely on theoretical concepts, "Industry 4.0 Revolution" takes a hands-on approach to exploring Industry 4.0. Through real-world case studies and examples, readers gain practical insights into how leading companies are leveraging digital technologies to drive innovation, improve efficiency, and stay competitive in today's fast-paced market.

- *Thought Leadership*: Authored by an industry expert with years of experience in manufacturing and digital transformation, "Industry 4.0 Revolution" is a testament to the thought leadership and expertise of its author. By sharing their insights, strategies, and lessons learned, the author empowers readers to take proactive steps towards embracing Industry 4.0 and shaping the future of manufacturing.

In summary, "Industry 4.0 Revolution: How Startups Empower Digital Transformation in Industries" is not just a book—it's a roadmap to success in the digital age. Whether you're looking to gain a deeper understanding of Industry 4.0, explore new opportunities for growth, or stay ahead of the competition, this book is your guide to navigating the future of manufacturing.

To connect with the author and learn more about "Industry 4.0 Revolution: How Startups Empower Digital Transformation in Industries," visit his LinkedIn profile: Aeknath Mishra: LinkedIn

Feel free to reach out to them for further insights, discussions, or collaboration opportunities.

ASSESSMENT FOR INDUSTRY 4.0

Conducting an assessment or audit to determine readiness for Industry 4.0 implementation involves evaluating various aspects of your organization's current operations, technological infrastructure, and workforce capabilities. Here are steps to conduct such an assessment:

Q:	Define Objectives?
A:	
Q:	Establish Assessment Team?
A:	
Q:	Identify Key Stakeholders?
A:	
Q:	Conduct Gap Analysis?
A:	
Q:	Assess Technology Infrastructure?
A:	
Q:	Evaluate Data Management Processes?

A:	
Q:	Analyze Workforce Skills?
A:	
Q:	Assess Organizational Culture?
A:	
Q:	Review Regulatory Compliance?
A:	
Q:	Benchmark Against Industry Standards?
A:	
Q:	Develop Action Plan?
A:	
Q:	Monitor and Adjust?
A:	

By following these steps, organizations can conduct effective assessments and audits to determine their readiness for Industry 4.0 implementation and develop actionable strategies to drive successful digital transformation initiatives.

Assessment guidelines

- **Define Objectives:** Clearly define the objectives of the assessment, including understanding the potential benefits of Industry 4.0 adoption, identifying areas for improvement, and setting specific goals for digital transformation.

- **Establish Assessment Team:** Form a cross-functional team comprising representatives from different departments, including operations, IT, engineering, and human resources, to ensure comprehensive coverage and diverse perspectives.

- **Identify Key Stakeholders:** Identify key stakeholders, including senior management, department heads, and frontline employees, whose input and involvement are crucial for the success of the assessment.

- **Conduct Gap Analysis:** Evaluate your organization's current state by conducting a gap analysis to identify discrepancies between your existing capabilities and the requirements of Industry 4.0. Assess factors such as technology infrastructure, data management processes, workforce skills, and organizational culture.

- **Assess Technology Infrastructure:** Evaluate your current technology infrastructure, including hardware, software systems, and networking capabilities, to determine its readiness for supporting Industry 4.0 technologies such as IoT, automation, cloud computing, and data analytics.

- **Evaluate Data Management Processes:** Assess your organization's data management processes, including data collection, storage, analysis, and security practices. Determine the availability, quality, and accessibility of data required for implementing Industry 4.0 initiatives.

- **Analyze Workforce Skills:** Evaluate the skills and competencies of your workforce to determine their readiness to adopt and utilize new technologies associated with Industry 4.0. Identify gaps in skills and training needs for upskilling and reskilling employees.

- **Assess Organizational Culture**: Evaluate your organization's culture, including its openness to change, willingness to experiment, and commitment to innovation. Identify cultural barriers or resistance to digital transformation initiatives and develop strategies to address them.

- **Review Regulatory Compliance:** Assess regulatory compliance requirements relevant to your industry and region, including data privacy, cybersecurity, and industry-specific standards. Ensure that Industry 4.0 initiatives comply with applicable regulations and standards.

- **Benchmark Against Industry Standards:** Compare your organization's readiness against industry benchmarks and best practices for Industry 4.0 adoption. Consider factors such as technological maturity, market trends, and competitive landscape to gauge your organization's position.

- **Develop Action Plan:** Based on the findings of the assessment, develop a comprehensive action plan outlining specific initiatives, timelines, responsibilities, and resource requirements for implementing Industry 4.0 solutions. Prioritize initiatives based on their impact and feasibility.

- **Monitor and Adjust:** Continuously monitor the progress of Industry 4.0 implementation initiatives and regularly review and adjust the action plan based on feedback, changing requirements, and emerging opportunities. Stay agile and adaptive to ensure successful digital transformation.

EVALUATING DIGITAL TRANSFORMATION NEEDS

Questionnaires to evaluate, assess, and recommend Industry 4.0 solutions for a manufacturing company:

General Information:

Q: What is the size and scale of your manufacturing operations?

A:

Q: What products do you manufacture, and what is your production capacity?

A:

Q: How many employees are currently working in your manufacturing facility?

A:

Current Technological Infrastructure:

Q: What technology systems and equipment are currently in place in your manufacturing facility?

A:

Q:	Do you have any existing automation or digitalization initiatives?
A:	
Q:	What software applications are you currently using for production, inventory management, and quality control?
A:	

Industry 4.0 Readiness Assessment:

Q:	How familiar are you with the concept of Industry 4.0?
A:	
Q:	Have you conducted any assessments or audits to determine your readiness for Industry 4.0 implementation?
A:	
Q:	What are your main objectives or goals for adopting Industry 4.0 technologies?
A:	

Specific Needs and Challenges:

Q:	What are the main pain points or challenges in your current manufacturing processes?
A:	
Q:	What areas of your operations do you believe could benefit the most from digitalization and automation?
A:	
Q:	Are there any specific regulatory or compliance requirements that need to be addressed?
A:	

INDUSTRY 4.0 REVOLUTION

Budget and Resources:

Q: What is your budget for implementing Industry 4.0 solutions?

A:

Q: Do you have dedicated resources or personnel available for managing and implementing digital transformation initiatives?

A:

Q: Are you open to investing in training and upskilling your workforce to adapt to new technologies?

A:

Integration and Scalability:

Q: How important is it for the proposed solutions to integrate seamlessly with your existing systems and equipment?

A:

Q: Are you looking for solutions that can scale as your business grows or changes?

A:

Data Security and Privacy:

Q: How concerned are you about data security and privacy when adopting Industry 4.0 technologies?

A:

Q: What measures do you currently have in place to protect sensitive data and intellectual property?

A:

Vendor Selection Criteria:

Q:	What criteria are important to you when selecting vendors or solution providers for Industry 4.0 implementation?
A:	
Q:	Are you open to working with multiple vendors or prefer a single integrated solution provider?
A:	

Return on Investment (ROI) Expectations:

Q:	What ROI expectations do you have for the proposed Industry 4.0 initiatives?
A:	
Q:	How do you plan to measure the success and impact of these initiatives on your business?
A:	

Long term strategy:

Q:	What is your long-term vision for digital transformation and Industry 4.0 in your organization?
A:	
Q:	How do you plan to stay agile and adapt to future technological advancements and industry trends?
A:	

These questions can help gather important information to assess the current state of the manufacturing company, identify specific needs and challenges, and recommend suitable Industry 4.0 solutions tailored to their requirements.

DIGITAL TRANSFORMATION RESOURCES

The list of digital transformation tools, technologies, APIs, and companies available in the market, aligned with the various aspects of Industry 4.0 implementation discussed earlier are as:

1	Automation and Robotics	• Robotics Process Automation (RPA) platforms: UiPath, Automation Anywhere, Blue Prism. • Industrial robots: ABB, Fanuc, Yaskawa. • Collaborative robots (cobots): Universal Robots, Rethink Robotics, KUKA.
2	Internet of Things (IoT) and Predictive Analytics	• IoT platforms: Microsoft Azure IoT, AWS IoT, IBM Watson IoT.

		• Industrial IoT sensors and devices: Siemens, Bosch, Schneider Electric.
3	Predictive analytics software	SAS Analytics, IBM SPSS, RapidMiner
4	Data Analytics	• Business Intelligence (BI) tools: Tableau, Power BI, QlikView • Data visualization libraries: D3.js, Plotly, Matplotlib • Big data platforms: Apache Hadoop, Apache Spark, Google BigQuery
5	Supply Chain Optimization	• Supply chain management (SCM) software: SAP SCM, Oracle SCM, Infor SCM • Transportation management systems (TMS): MercuryGate, Manhattan Associates, Oracle Transportation Management • Warehouse management systems (WMS): Manhattan Associates, Blue Yonder (formerly JDA), Oracle WMS Cloud.
6	Digital Twin Technology	• Digital twin platforms: Siemens Digital Twin, PTC ThingWorx, IBM Watson IoT Platform

7	Cloud Computing	• Simulation and modeling software: Ansys, COMSOL Multiphysics, SimScale. • Cloud service providers: Amazon Web Services (AWS), Microsoft Azure, Google Cloud Platform (GCP) • Cloud-based enterprise resource planning (ERP) systems: SAP S/4HANA Cloud, Oracle ERP Cloud, Microsoft Dynamics 365.
8	Blockchain Integration	• Blockchain platforms: Ethereum, Hyperledger Fabric, Corda • Supply chain blockchain solutions: IBM Food Trust, VeChain, ShipChain
9	Augmented Reality (AR) and Virtual Reality (VR)	• AR development platforms: Unity, Vuforia, ARKit (for iOS), ARCore (for Android) • VR headsets and devices: Oculus Rift, HTC Vive, PlayStation VR.
10	Smart Manufacturing	• Industrial IoT platforms: Siemens MindSphere, GE Predix, Hitachi Lumada

		• Manufacturing execution systems (MES): Aegis, Plex Systems, Wonderware MES.
11	Digital Workforce Enablement	• Learning management systems (LMS): Cornerstone OnDemand, Moodle, SAP Litmos • Digital skills training platforms: Udemy for Business, Coursera for Business, LinkedIn Learning
12	Regulatory Compliance	• Compliance management software: MetricStream, ComplianceQuest, ZenGRC • Cybersecurity solutions: Palo Alto Networks, Fortinet, Check Point Software
13	Industry 4.0 Consulting and Integration	• Accenture • Deloitte • PwC (PricewaterhouseCoopers) • Capgemini • IBM Global Business Services

These tools, technologies and companies provide a wide range of solutions and services to support organizations in their digital transformation journey towards Industry 4.0 implementation.

API Files for Digital Transformation

In the context of Industry 4.0, API Files act as crucial digital interfaces that facilitate seamless communication and data exchange among diverse manufacturing systems, including those in the steel and aluminium sectors, as well as their supporting vendors and software applications. By adhering to these guidelines, industrious startup founders can engage in collaborative brainstorming to innovate and implement highly efficient, interconnected manufacturing processes, thereby driving significant advancements and achieving operational excellence across the industry.

The author delineates the descriptions, features, and website addresses for API files pertinent to various Digital Transformation departments. To harness these frameworks effectively in Industry 4.0 applications, practitioners must typically develop bespoke code to define endpoints, manage data ingestion, conduct model training, perform inference, and execute analytics aligned with specific requirements and business logic. These frameworks offer the essential foundation and tools for implementing APIs, yet necessitate customization and integration with IT models and data sources from operational technology (OT) to achieve seamless digital transformation.

Artificial Intelligence and Machine Learning

Website: **TensorFlow Serving**

Description: TensorFlow Serving is an open-source serving system specifically designed for deploying machine learning models. It allows you to serve models built with TensorFlow as APIs, making it easier to integrate machine learning into production environments.

Website: **TorchServe** (PyTorch Serving)

Description: PyTorch Serving is similar to TensorFlow Serving but tailored for models built with PyTorch. It allows you to deploy PyTorch models as APIs, providing a streamlined approach to putting PyTorch models into production.

Website: **FastAPI**

Description: FastAPI is a modern, fast (high-performance) web framework for building APIs with Python 3.7+ based on standard Python type hints. It is designed to be easy to use while being highly efficient.

Website: **Flask**

Description: Flask is a lightweight WSGI web application framework in Python.

These tools provide the foundation and utilities necessary to develop and deploy APIs for AI and machine learning models within the context of digital transformation in Industry 4.0. They offer flexibility, scalability, and integration capabilities that are crucial for building robust and efficient systems that leverage AI and machine learning for industrial applications.

Data Analytics or big data

Website: **Apache Kafka**

Description: Apache Kafka is a distributed streaming platform that can be used for building real-time data pipelines and streaming applications.

Website: **Apache Spark**

Description: Apache Spark is an open-source unified analytics engine for large-scale data processing.

Website: **Elasticsearch**

Description: Elasticsearch is a distributed, RESTful search and analytics engine designed for horizontal scalability, reliability, and real-time search capabilities.

Website: **Apache Druid**

Description: Apache Druid is a high-performance, real-time analytics database designed for fast data ingestion and queries on large datasets.

INDUSTRY 4.0 REVOLUTION

Automation and Robotics

Website: **ROS** (Robot Operating System):

Description: ROS is a flexible framework for writing robot software. It is not just a single API but a collection of tools, libraries, and conventions to simplify the task of creating complex and robust robot behavior.

Website: **OpenAI Gym**

Description: OpenAI Gym is a toolkit for developing and comparing reinforcement learning algorithms. While not strictly an API for robotics control, it provides environments and interfaces that can be used to simulate and control robotic systems in a virtual environment.

Website: **MoveIt!**

Description: MoveIt! is a widely-used open-source software for motion planning, manipulation, and control of robotic systems. It is primarily used with ROS but provides its own set of APIs and tools for robot control.

Website: **Apache PLC4X**

Description: Apache PLC4X is an open-source project that provides a set of libraries for communicating with industrial programmable logic controllers (PLCs) and automation devices.

These tools and frameworks provide the foundational components and APIs necessary for building and integrating automation and robotics solutions within the context of Industry 4.0.

IOT and Predictive Analytics

Creating API files for IoT and Predictive Analytics in the context of Digital Transformation in Industry 4.0 involves designing endpoints that handle data ingestion from IoT devices, perform real-time analytics, and enable predictive maintenance and insights generation. Here's a conceptual outline of four API files for this purpose:

Website: **Apache Kafka**

Description: Apache Kafka is a distributed streaming platform that can handle high-throughput, real-time data ingestion from IoT devices.

Website: **Apache Flink**

Description: Apache Flink is an open-source stream processing framework with powerful event-time processing capabilities.

Website: **InfluxDB**

Description: InfluxDB is an open-source time series database designed to handle high-write and query loads.

Website: **Grafana**

Description: Grafana is an open-source analytics and monitoring platform designed for visualizing time series data.

These tools provide the infrastructure and capabilities necessary to build and deploy APIs for handling IoT data ingestion, real-time analytics, predictive maintenance, and visualization in Industry 4.0 environments.

Supply chain with Blockchain

Website: **Hyperledger Fabric**

Description: Hyperledger Fabric is a permissioned blockchain framework implementation and one of the Hyperledger projects hosted by The Linux Foundation.

Website: **Hyperledger Sawtooth**

Description: Hyperledger Sawtooth is another blockchain platform under the Hyperledger umbrella, designed for building distributed ledger applications and networks.

Website: **Ethereum**

Description: Ethereum is a decentralized platform that runs smart contracts, which are applications that run exactly as programmed without any possibility of downtime, fraud, censorship, or third-party interference.

Website: **Quorum GitHub**

Description: Quorum is an open-source blockchain platform that combines the innovation of Ethereum with enhancements to support enterprise needs. It is maintained by ConsenSys.

These platforms provide the foundational tools and capabilities needed to integrate blockchain technology into supply chain applications for Industry 4.0.

Digital Twin Technology
Website: **FIWARE**

Description: FIWARE is an open-source platform that provides a set of APIs and components for building smart solutions in various domains, including Digital Twins.

Website: **Eclipse Ditto**

Description: Eclipse Ditto is an open-source framework for creating and managing Digital Twins. It is part of the Eclipse IoT project.

Website: **ThingWorx**

Description: ThingWorx, owned by PTC, is an Industrial IoT platform that includes capabilities for creating and managing Digital Twins.

Website: **Digital Twin Consortium**

Description: The DTC Reference Model is a set of guidelines and standards for building and interoperating Digital Twins across different industries.

These platforms and frameworks provide the foundational capabilities and tools necessary to build and deploy Digital Twin applications in Industry 4.0 contexts.

Cloud Computing

Website: **OpenStack**

Description: OpenStack is a cloud computing platform that provides infrastructure as a service (IaaS) for deploying and managing virtual machines, containers, and other cloud resources.

Website: **Kubernetes** (K8s)

Description: Kubernetes is an open-source container orchestration platform for automating the deployment, scaling, and management of containerized applications.

Website: **Apache Mesos**

Description: Apache Mesos is an open-source cluster manager that simplifies the deployment and management of applications in large-scale clustered environments.

Website: **Cloud Foundry**

Description: Cloud Foundry is an open-source platform as a service (PaaS) that enables developers to deploy, manage, and scale applications quickly and easily.

These platforms and frameworks provide the foundational tools and APIs necessary for leveraging Cloud Computing Technology in Industry 4.0 environments.

Smart Manufacturing

Website: **OPC Foundation** (Open Platform Communications Unified Architecture):

Description: OPC UA is a standard for industrial communication and interoperability, widely used in smart manufacturing for data exchange between machines and enterprise systems.

Website: **Node-RED**

Description: Node-RED is an open-source visual programming tool for wiring together hardware devices, APIs, and online services.

Website: **Eclipse IoT** - Eclipse IoT Packages (Kura, Kapua, Hono)

Description: Eclipse IoT projects provide a range of tools and frameworks for building IoT and smart manufacturing solutions.

Features: Projects like Eclipse Kura (for edge computing), Eclipse Kapua (for IoT device management), and Eclipse Hono (for IoT messaging) offer APIs and services that facilitate device connectivity, data management, and application integration in manufacturing environments.

Website: **Apache PLC4X**

Description: Apache PLC4X is an open-source set of libraries for communicating with industrial programmable logic controllers (PLCs) and other industrial devices.

These platforms and tools provide the foundational capabilities and APIs necessary for implementing Smart Manufacturing Technology in Industry 4.0 environments. They support connectivity, data exchange, automation, and integration with enterprise systems, enabling organizations to enhance productivity, optimize processes, and achieve digital transformation goals effectively.

Digital Workforce

To support the implementation of these APIs, here are some open-source tools and platforms commonly used for building and managing digital workforce technologies:

Website: **Camunda BPM**

Description: Camunda BPM is an open-source platform for workflow and business process management.

API Documentation: Camunda BPM REST API

Website: **Robocorp**

Description: Robocorp provides open-source tools for robotic process automation (RPA).

API Documentation: Robocorp API Documentation

Website: **Rocket.Chat**

Description: Rocket.Chat is an open-source communication and collaboration platform.

API Documentation: Rocket.Chat REST API

Website: **Metabase**

Description: Metabase is an open-source business intelligence and analytics platform.

API Documentation: Metabase API Documentation

These open-source platforms provide robust APIs to support the development and management of Digital Workforce Technology, enabling automation, workflow management, communication, collaboration, and performance analytics in Industry 4.0 environments.

ABOUT THE AUTHOR

Aeknath Mishra, a startup enthusiast, exemplifies the seamless intersection of experience and youthful enthusiasm in the realm of literature. His collaborative journey in the world of writing is a testament to the power of shared passions, diverse perspectives, and unwavering dedication. He preferred to be private, vibe alone, and grow in silence.

Aeknath Mishra, with his extensive background in the industry, brings a wealth of experience to the table. Having served in esteemed organizations such as Tata Steel, Aluminium Bahrain, and Emirates Global Aluminium, Aeknath has honed his skills and expertise over decades of dedicated service. His journey in the manufacturing sector has been nothing short of remarkable, marked by numerous achievements, milestones, and invaluable learnings along the way. Throughout his illustrious career, Aeknath has been instrumental in driving innovation, fostering growth, and shaping the future of the industry.

With a keen eye for detail and a passion for storytelling, Aeknath embarked on a mission to share his insights and experiences with the world through the medium of literature. His vision to publish 40 books stands as a testament to his unwavering commitment to knowledge sharing and lifelong learning. Each book represents a unique narrative, a trove of wisdom, and a legacy of excellence that transcends generations. Aeknath's dedication to his craft, coupled with his boundless curiosity and thirst for knowledge, serves as an inspiration to aspiring writers, startup founders, and industry professionals alike.

Aeknath Mishra represents a dynamic cadre of writers, each bringing their unique strengths, insights, and perspectives to the table. The collaborative efforts transcend generational boundaries, bridging the gap between experience and youth, tradition and innovation. Through a shared passion for literature and storytelling, Aeknath strives to create a legacy of excellence that will endure for generations to come.

In conclusion, the journey of Aeknath Mishra serves as a testament to the transformative power of literature, the enduring bond between generations, and the limitless potential of collaboration. As he continues to chart new territories, explore new ideas, and inspire others with his writing, Aeknath embodies the essence of creativity, curiosity, and camaraderie that defines the world of literature.

REFERENCES

1	Smart Manufacturing: Innovation and Transformation by Yusuf Altıntepe
2	Start with Why: How Great Leaders Inspire Everyone to Take Action by Simon Sinek
3	The Innovator's Dilemma: When New Technologies Cause Great Firms to Fail by Clayton M. Christensen
4	The Startup Way: How Modern Companies Use Entrepreneurial Management to Transform Culture and Drive Long-Term Growth by Eric Ries
5	Augmented Reality: Principles and Practice by Dieter Schmalstieg and Tobias Hollerer
6	Blockchain Basics: A Non-Technical Introduction in 25 Steps by Daniel Drescher
7	Supply Chain Management for Dummies by Daniel Stanton
8	The Lean Startup: How Today's Entrepreneurs Use Continuous Innovation to Create Radically Successful Businesses by Eric Ries
9	Future-Ready Leadership Strategies for the Fourth Industrial Revolution by Chris R. Groscurth
10	Cloud Computing: Concepts, Technology & Architecture - Thomas Erl, Ricardo Puttini, and Zaigham Mahmood
11	Digital Twin Technologies and Smart Cities - Abhishek Kumar and Vishal Jain
12	Myopic Startup: The Mistakes You Made Which Are Killing Your Success by Aeknath Mishra

13	Juan : The Dilemma of Being Born into Poverty by Aeknath Mishra
14	Business Success Checklist: A Handbook for Visionary Leaders to Make Critical Business Decisions Easy by Aeknath Mishra
15	Karate Kudos: Learning Shotokan way of martial arts by Tamanna Mishra
16	Profiting from Industry 4.0: The road to future value in manufacturing by Marcos Kauffman
17	What is Industry 4.0 by IBM - www.ibm.com/topics/industry-4-0
18	What is industry 4.0 and the Fourth Industrial Revolution by McKinsey
19	Fourth Industrial Revolution from www.wikipedia.org/wiki/Fourth_Industrial_Revolution
20	Industry 4.0: The Future of Manufacturing by SAP
21	Youthquake 4.0: A Whole Generation and the new industrial Revolution by Rocky Scopelliti
22	The Fourth Industrial Revolution by Klaus Schwab

INDUSTRY 4.0 REVOLUTION

References – 36 Startup's

	Technology	Company
1	Celestial Manufacturing Solutions	www.h2greensteel.com
2	Cobot Auto Tech	www.anybotics.com
3	Predicti Tech	www.facilio.com
4	Data Matrix	www.mavenintel.com
5	Logic Chain	www.synox.io
6	Emirates Twin Makers	www.intemic.com
7	Cloud Fab	www.rapyder.com
8	Blockcom Supply	www.scorechain.com
9	Virtual Fab	www.aruvr.com
10	Smart Grid Systems	www.discover.aveva.com
11	Skill Shift	www.daon.com
12	Cyber Guard	www.orro.group.com
13	Energy Plus	www.greensoftware.foundation
14	Green Cycle	www.hydro.com
15	Sedaro digital twins	www.sedaro.com
16	MediLedger Network	www.mediledger.com
17	Oneway Robotics	www.onewayrobot.com
18	HalZero technology	www.hydro.com
19	Novelis Recycling aluminium	www.novelis.com
20	Rio Tinto Energy Efficiency	www.arena.gov.au

21	BMW Digital Light Synthesis	www.carbon3d.com
22	GE 3D-printed jet engine	www.ge.com
23	Siemens energy trading	www.lo3energy.com
24	Nike 3D printing	www.press.siemens.com
25	Toyota - TRI-AD	www.preferred.jp
26	Toyota EV & Plug-in Hybrid	www.global.toyota/en
27	Airbus Cargo Drone	www.airbus.com
28	Siemens carbon capture tech	www.carbonclean.com
29	Alcoa recycled CO_2	www.carboncure.com
30	ArcelorMittal procurement	www.xometry.asia
31	Novelis EV batteries	www.ampcera.com
32	Norsk Hydro solar power	www.heliogen.com
33	Tata Steel components printing	www.velo3d.com
34	BALCO Face & mood detection	www.entropik.io
35	JSW Steel Conveyor Monitor	www.zestiot.com
36	Rio Tinto Iron and RTIT	www.riotinto.com

BOOKS BY AEKNATH MISHRA

Elevate your Reading

Scan this QR to buy them

Read here

www.ingramcontent.com/pod-product-compliance
Lightning Source LLC
Chambersburg PA
CBHW071925210526
45479CB00002B/554